ANTIQUE GLASS AND CHINA

ANTIQUE GLASS AND CHINA

Guide for the Beginning Collector

y Geoffrey A. Godden

ASTLE BOOKS ★ NEW YORK

This edition published by arrangement with
A. S. BARNES AND CO., INC.

Printed in the United States of America

To Jeanie and all new collectors

CONTENTS

ACKNOWLEDGEMENTS

I acknowledge with gratitude the help given to me in the preparation of this book by specialized dealers and collectors and the generous assistance I have received from Librarians and Museum Curators to whom I have written to check facts on their local wares and personages.

Much information has been obtained from 19th century copies of the trade journal *Pottery Gazette and Glass Trade Review* (published by Scott, Greenwood & Son Ltd); interesting advertisements have been reproduced from this source. Plate 29 is of objects in the British Museum (Crown Copyright). The photographs of Clarke's Fairy lights are copies of a series in the possession of the Corning Museum of Glass, Corning, New York, USA.

Other photographs, unless otherwise stated, are from the stock of Messrs Godden of Worthing Ltd or from my own collection. These latter photographs were all taken by Derek Gardiner A.I.B.P.

INTRODUCTORY NOTES

THIS IS not intended to be a general 'chatty' book; my intention has been to write a serious reference book giving factual information on the less expensive British china and glass wares that are generally neglected in books dealing with more sophisticated and expensive objects. Many quotations have been included and these have been obtained from 'out of the way' sources.

The reader will be introduced to a selection of wares that have interest and decorative value. All these objects can be found in fair numbers at the present time and the search for them should make a holiday, or retirement, all the more enjoyable.

The price range I have had in mind as being suitable for collectors on a small budget is from one to five pounds,* obviously the range of such objects is restricted to small items but this is often an advantage. With careful buying, good specimens of all wares mentioned in this book can be purchased for under five pounds at the present time – a single showcase will house one's complete collection. One of the main objects in writing this book is to suggest to the prospective collector that it is far better to collect good specimens of neglected and perhaps not strictly 'antique' objects, than it is to collect poor, damaged and repaired specimens of the more fashionable collector's wares.

As the prices for antiques increase, as they have done on an increasing scale in recent years, the new collector with limited resources, seeking an absorbing hobby, must either collect second-rate expensive objects or seek out a new subject to collect. There can be no doubt which of these alternatives will prove the most rewarding.

To many collectors the word 'antique' would seem to have magic qualities. They ask 'is it antique' when they should ask themselves 'is it of good quality'. The general definition of an antique is an object over one hundred years old but age does not make a bad object good. A poorly designed, bad quality piece of china ninety-nine years old does not become well designed and good quality when it has been in existence for a further year. Several of the classes of collectable objects discussed in this book are not strictly speaking 'antiques'. This is in keeping with my belief that quality, interest and decorative value should be considered above age.

The question of price and value will worry many collectors. If a collector is going to be obsessed with this question, he should confine his interests to stocks and shares. The collecting of antiques should be regarded as an interesting hobby which will bring many years of pleasure. This is not to say that a collection cannot be sold at a profit; there are few collectors that have not sold their acquisitions at an enhanced price but this must not be the main concern while the collection is being formed.

The cost of an acquisiton has no relation to the joy and interest that its discovery and purchase can bestow. The purchase of an object for one pound can give the real collector much more pleasure than the purchase of an 'objet d'art' by a millionaire for tens of thousands of pounds. In the latter case the purchase was probably made through the unromantic hands of an agent entrusted to buy any suitable object as soon as it appears on the market; there was little or no joy in the search, simply the ability to pay the price. This is not the way to *enjoy* collecting.

*American readers should not presume that they can purchase in their own country the objects mentioned in this book at, or below, the dollar equivalent of five pounds or any other Sterling price quoted.

Apart from the modest profit due to the American dealer, the cost of transport, plus the Customs duty and many other legitimate expenses, considerably increase the price.

Geoffrey A. Godden,
14, Sompting Avenue,
Worthing, Sussex,
England.

ANTIQUE GLASS AND CHINA

CHAPTER ONE

COLLECTING MARKS AND
PRINTED EARTHENWARES

FOR SEVERAL years I have received curious looks from shop-keepers when I explained that I was looking for unusual marks. There was a very good reason for my interest, in that I was trying to trace all known marks for inclusion in a new comprehensive mark book* and in connection with this project I was endeavouring to form a collection of documentary pieces bearing these marks.

The formation of the collection has proved of the greatest interest and has resulted in the rediscovery of several hitherto unrecorded potters. The wares of the smaller manufacturers can have charm and, as the small firms were often of short duration, their wares can often be dated to narrow limits. As a general rule the neglected wares of the minor 19th-century potters can be purchased for under five pounds, although very fine or important specimens will command a higher price.

Before making some suggestions for the collection of suitable marked wares, it would be beneficial to give some general notes on forms of marks, and the methods by which they can be attributed.

Antique ceramic marks are applied in three basic ways; they are impressed in the soft body before firing, printed (either under or over the glaze) during the process of decoration, or painted by hand during or after decoration. The printed marks will be found to outnumber all others. Examples decorated with blue underglaze subjects – such as the well-known Willow pattern will be found to bear blue underglaze marks, and pieces with overglaze prints, often in black, will have overglaze marks.

* *Encyclopaedia of British Pottery and Porcelain Marks.*

The reason for this is that the engraved copper plate from which the design was transferred to the article, by means of tissue-like paper, also bore the maker's mark and as the main design was applied to the face of the object to be decorated, the mark was cut off and transferred to the underside and so was in the same colour as the main design.

The marks themselves will be found to give the maker's name in full or his initials or a trade sign or crest device, or will only comprise the name of the pattern or type of body – Ironstone, Pearl ware, etc. The marks incorporating initials are by far the most frequent and interesting. They afford the collector the opportunity for research into contemporary records, directories, rate lists, etc., in order to link the initials with a manufacturer of the correct period. In some cases this cannot be an exact science for several initials or combinations of initials fit many firms. The initials 'B. & B.' fit thirty-two Staffordshire firms! Other sets of initials only relate to one firm – W.D.C. to William D. Chesworth, Upper High Street, Hanley (c. 1845); W. & G.H. to William and George Harding, Furlong Pottery, Burslem (1851–5); W.R.S. & Co. to William Ridgway, Son & Co., Church Works, Hanley (1838–48), to give only three examples.

Even when many firms fit one set of initials, the list can be narrowed down, either by fixing the correct period or by locating the town of manufacture. Most collectors will have some idea if the shape or design of an object is pre-Victorian, or early or late Victorian and so can concentrate their search among the manufacturers of that period. The form of mark can often help to date an example. Very many 19th-century marks incorporate the Royal Arms: the pre-Victorian examples engraved before

1837 will show an inescutcheon or small shield at the centre of the Royal Arms, the Victorian Arms show simple quartered arms. I am often surprised by serious collectors who show me examples bearing plain Victorian post-1837 Royal Arms which are attributed by their owners to the 1810s and 1820s. Many printed initial marks were incorporated in a circular or oval garter-like mark to which a crown was sometimes added; this form was not used before the 1840s. The collector will be able to discover many other basic forms of marks that would seem to have been fashionable for short periods and therefore give an approximate guide to the date.

Other general guides to dating ceramic marks will be found useful and will save many serious errors.

1. Printed or other marks incorporating the Royal Arms are 19th century or later.
2. Any printed mark incorporating the name of the pattern may be regarded as subsequent to 1810.
3. The use of 'Limited' or its abbreviations – 'Ltd' 'Ld', etc., after a firm's title or initials denotes a date after 1860 and was in fact very rarely used before 1880.
4. The use of the word 'Royal' in the manufacturer's title or trade name suggests a date after the middle of the 19th century.
5. The incorporation of the words 'Trade Mark' signifies a date after the Trade Mark Act of 1862.
6. The inclusion of the word 'England' indicates a date after 1875 and in most cases this word was added to marks from 1891 to comply with the American McKinley Tariff Act, which required the country of origin to be stamped on all imported wares. The term 'Made in England' points to a 20th-century dating.
7. The words 'Bone China' or 'English Bone China' denote a 20th-century date.

Having narrowed down the period of an initial mark, it is often possible to trace the town in which the potter was situated. In some cases the town is given in full as with the mark of Messrs Skinner and Walker of Stockton-on-Tees, Yorkshire:

S. & W.
STOCKTON.

This saves one attributing their wares to one of the nine Staffordshire firms with these initials. Several marks will be found to have initials arranged in triangular form

B. & B.   or   F. & R.
L.   B.

In these cases the lower initial relates to the town in the Staffordshire Potteries in which the firm was situated. This information can be of the greatest assistance in tracing a manufacturer or in rejecting other firms of the same initials but with different addresses. The main initials B, C, F, H, L, S & T stand for Burslem, Cobridge, Fenton, Hanley, Longton, Stoke and Tunstall, all of which make up the 'Staffordshire Potteries'.

Most mark books will be found rather unhelpful to the collector of the wares of the small, little-known potters for these books are in the main concerned with fashionable wares and include only a small proportion of known marks, quite often with a large proportion of errors of fact! It was to remedy this situation that I set out to collect marks and prepare a new comprehensive mark book which would be founded on documentary evidence rather than on earlier books.

Of the several small mark books now on the market John Cushion's *Pocket Book of English Ceramic Marks* is by far the most reliable, though by no means comprehensive or without error. The collector's 'bible', Chaffers *Marks and Monograms on European and Oriental Pottery and Porcelain*, is more than a mark book as it contains a full and interesting text on the history and products of each firm. The latest revised 15th edition has corrected many of the serious errors that occurred in earlier editions and which were repeated in other books.

Apart from the obvious course of collecting the printed patterns that attract you regardless of the maker or period, I would suggest for the inquiring collector who enjoys seeking new information and adding to our general knowledge of English ceramics that he should seek out and study the wares of hitherto unknown makers. For a very small outlay one can form a most interesting collection of 'unknown' wares. Three weeks ago in Tunbridge Wells, while looking for unusual marks, I discovered an earthenware mug decorated with an amusing print of children playing soldiers (see Plate 1). The printed mark on the base read: 'Industrial Pottery. Bo'ness'. I could not trace the pottery in the standard reference books and the authorities at the Royal Scottish Museum, Edinburgh had no record of the existence of such a concern. Local Librarians are usually most helpful in tracing potters in their local directories, etc., and in this case the Edinburgh City Librarian, Mr C. S. Minto, was able to find for me the 'Industrial Co-operative Pottery Society' of Grange Pans, Bo'ness in a Directory of 1893. Apart from this reference the Bo'ness Industrial Pottery does not seem to be recorded, but the Edinburgh Registrar of Friendly Societies has informed me that his records show that the parent concern was registered in December 1887 under the title 'Bo'ness Industrial Pottery & Manufacturing Society'. It was changed in January 1892 to the Industrial Co-operative Pottery Society Limited, but in February 1894 an order was made to wind-up this short-lived Scottish pottery. This is the sort of information on little or unknown factories that the enterprising collector can unearth for himself.

In Oxford I found quite by chance in a very good class Antique shop dealing in Oriental and early English wares a 19th-century transfer printed plate with a floral moulded border. This attractive plate (see Plate 2) which cost twenty-five shillings, bears the hitherto unrecorded impressed name mark 'J. CARR & Co'. The Staffordshire rate records, of which I have transcriptions, do not record any potter of this name but after interesting research I discovered that this firm worked the Low Lights Pottery at North Shields, Northumberland. With the help of the City Librarian at Newcastle-upon-Tyne I have been able to ascertain that local directories list the following changes in the owners of the Low Lights Pottery: Carr and Patton in 1841; John Carr in 1847; John Carr & Co. (as on my marked plate) in 1850; John Carr & Son in 1854 and John Carr & Sons from 1861. Here then is an example (and by no means an isolated example) of an inexpensive piece adding to our knowledge of English pottery and giving its purchaser interest in the process.

The patriotic collector can specialize in the wares of his country or district. The London stoneware factories of the 19th-century are neglected. The several potteries of the Sunderland district are well worth study. A booklet entitled *The Potteries of Sunderland and District* and edited by J. T. Shaw, A.L.A., the Director of Sunderland Museum & Art Gallery, is an indispensable guide to the varied wares made in and around the town. The Scottish potters also made interesting wares (most of which are unmarked); the standard reference book is J. Arnold Fleming's *Scottish Pottery* (1923). Information on many smaller potteries throughout the British Isles can be found in L. Jewitt's *The Ceramic Art of Great Britain* (1878 and 1883 editions).

The collector of ceramic marks will soon discover that there are several marks of the same basic form to which different initials have been added. The reason for this is that many of the smaller manufacturers purchased their designs from firms such as Green, Sargeant and Pepper of Hanley who specialized in designing printed patterns, engraving the copper plates and selling them to the potters. Often the same design was sold to different firms, with their relevant initials or name engraved into the standard mark. One popular pattern 'Asiatic Phea-

1. Late Victorian earthenwares printed with sporting subjects. The centre mug is from the Industrial Pottery, Bo'ness.

sants' was supplied to over twenty different firms and their name added to the ornate mark which always occurs on wares bearing this subject. The popular 'Pekin' pattern was also used by several firms and nearly always bears the same form of circular mark. Very many other instances of this practice could be cited and collections formed of individual patterns manufactured by different firms. Patterns such as the ever popular Willow pattern were made by hundreds of different potters from the 18th-century onwards; several variations are met with and many examples are marked and can be dated within narrow limits.

The collection of marks also makes it possible to collect the wares of one family of potters, or wares made by a potter of your own name. During the 1830s many decorative and interesting printed earthenwares were made in Staffordshire by potters named Godwin. These were Benjamin Godwin of Cobridge *c.* 1834–41; B. C. Godwin of Burslem *c.* 1851; John and Robert Godwin of Cobridge *c.* 1834–66; Godwin, Rowley & Co. of Burslem *c.* 1828–31; Thomas Godwin of Burslem *c.* 1834–54 and Thomas and Benjamin Godwin of Burslem *c.* 1809–34. All these potters produced good printed wares which are normally marked with their names or initials; examples are reasonably common and average specimens can be purchased for under five pounds. A representative selection is illustrated in Plate 3.

Most printed English earthenwares of the early 19th century were in the still popular underglaze blue of the typical Willow pattern type. The blue colour itself often offers a general guide to date, although the colour used by some individual potters tended to be characteristic and confined to their own products. In the 1810–20 period, the blue is of a medium dark shade; the 1820–30 period is darker but after 1830 it is of a decidedly lighter colour. The American market favoured a *very* dark blue in the 1815–30 period.

Many attractive printed patterns may be found in colours other than blue. Most authorities have stated that these other underglaze colours date from 1830 but in fact they were introduced in the late 1820s (some wares of the early 1800s occur printed in brown and other colours *over* the glaze). Simeon Shaw, in his *History of the Staffordshire Potteries* published in 1829 wrote – 'Very recently several of the most eminent Manufacturers have introduced a method of ornamenting Table and Dessert services, similarly to Tea Services, by the Black Printers using red, brown and green colours, for beautiful designs of flowers and landscapes . . . This pottery has a rich and delicate

appearance, and owing to the Blue printing having become so common, the other is now obtaining a decided preference in most genteel circles.'

This colour printed ware had arrived in America by 1830, for in this year Peter Morton of Hartford, Connecticut advertised:

'150 Crates and H. hds (Hogsheads) of China and Earthenware consisting of light blue, black, brown, pink and green printed Dining and Tea Ware'.

These printed wares can be most attractive and deserve more attention from the collector. It must not be thought that all

2. Printed plate with moulded border. Impressed mark 'J. Carr & Co.' *c.* 1850–4.

Selection of early Victorian printed pottery by the Godwins. Benjamin Godwin c. 1834–41; J. and R. Godwin c. 1834–66 and Thomas Godwin of Burslem (centre platter and 'Tam o'shanter' mug) c. 1834–54.

black and other colour printing dates from this period; *over*glaze printing in colour was a standard form of decoration used from the 18th century onwards.

Hundreds of English potters produced marked earthenwares of good quality during the 19th century. Their high standard was widely appreciated and the objects were exported all over the world in vast quantities. The Staffordshire potters produced special patterns for the overseas markets. The amount of blue printed earthenware shipped from England to North America is quite staggering. Many patterns depicted American views or historical subjects (see Plates 4 and 5). A dated advertisement (26 June 1826) issued by Peter Morton of Hartford, Connecticut includes an interesting reference to an American subject – a local observation tower:

'... 100 crates earthenware Ware, 60 of which have been just received per ship "Isaac Hicks" Liverpool, direct from the manufactory at Staffordshire, among which is an entirely new and most beautiful pattern of Tea Ware, called Wadsworth Tower ...'

This American-view Staffordshire pottery is avidly collected in America and several reference books have been published on the subject. It is both strange and sad that Staffordshire pottery

tions resist the action of the acid which eats into the unprotected parts giving a raised sunken pattern which can be used for printing in the normal way. This method of printing was used for applying printed pattern both on the biscuit ware, before glazing, and for overglaze work. Francis Morley (& Co.) of Broad Street, Shelton (*c.* 1845–58) was an early exponent of this technique and in 1848 Messrs Mintons were using this technique. In the 1860s several firms including Livesley, Powell & Co. of Hanley (*c.* 1851–66) developed this method of printing. An interesting contemporary reference to Livesley, Powell & Co. is contained in a French reference book of 1865 – 'They are now printing on stone by new processes that are still not very well known ... which give results that are superb for their fine quality, as for the clarity of the design.' With subsequent im-

bearing fine representations of English views, Country seats, etc., does not seem to be collected to any great extent in the country of its origin and the only comprehensive book on the subject *Anglo-American China, Part II* is by an American author, Sam Laidacker. Wake up English collectors! – these often inexpensive wares are seeped in history and are fine specimens of our ceramic art, not meant only for display but for everyday use and enjoyment.

An interesting but little-known type of ceramic printing was carried out by the Lithography process. Two Patents were taken out in 1839 by Pierre Auguste Ducote '... for improvements in printing china, porcelain, earthenware and other like wares ... by means of the design being drawn on Lithographic stone, which is then soaked in nitric acid'. The drawn, protected por-

provements mainly in the paper required for transferring the design from the etched stone to the ware, the lithographic process is still widely used in the industry today.

A related form of decoration by photographic processes is mentioned on page 64. I could continue giving examples of the vast untapped opportunities to be found in the close study of marks and among the wares of the neglected smaller potteries. However, I have probably already come near to bemusing the budding collector, and the specialist will find the fuller information he requires in the books I have mentioned and listed on page 92.

If an historian was asked to state in two hundred years' time the most significant contribution of the British Pottery industry to ceramic art, he might well suggest the high standard of the printed decoration applied to everyday useful products during the first half of the 19th century. The perfectionist will search for sharp clear impressions, printed from unworn copper plates, with the pigment fired at exactly the right temperature giving a good, strong, clean colour.

6. Rockingham type teaset registered by Samuel Alcock & Co of the Hill Pottery, Burslem, on June 14th, 1843. Creamer 4¾″ high.

CHAPTER TWO

REGISTRATION MARKS AND
REGISTERED PATTERNS

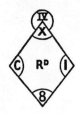

SEVERAL REFERENCES will be found later in this book to 'Registration Marks' or to 'Registered Patterns'. The 'Registration Mark' is always basically of diamond form (see example above). In the angles of the diamond various letters and figures appear, indicating the date when the design was first registered.

From 1797 various Acts sought to give copyright protection to original sculptured designs but it was not until 1839 that the designs had to be officially registered with the Board of Trade. In 1842 a new Act came into force 'applicable to the ornamenting of any article of manufacture . . . whether applicable to the pattern, or for the shape or configuration, or for the ornament thereof'. The 1842 Act divided the possible articles of manufacture into different classes which cover most aspects of Victorian art. The various classes were:

Class   i Ornamental designs in metal.
     ii Ornamental designs in wood.
    iii Ornamental designs in glass.
    iv Ornamental designs in earthenware (and porcelain), ivory, bone and other solid substances.

     v Ornamental designs – Paperhangings.
    vi Ornamental designs – Carpets, floor or oil cloth.
   vii Ornamental designs – Shawls – printed patterns.
  viii Ornamental designs – Shawls – patterns not printed.
    ix Yarn, thread – printed.
     x Woven fabrics – not furniture.
Class xi Woven fabrics – furniture, printed patterns.
    xii Woven fabrics – patterns not printed.
   xiii Lace and all other articles.

N.B. For the first six classes the design was protected for an initial period of three years.

All designs covered by registration were required to bear the diamond-shaped mark and from 1842 to 1883 hundreds of thousands of articles were made with this mark. Many of them can be purchased at little cost; extremely attractive ceramic designs can be found and a most instructive collection built up. It is possible to discover the day, month and year that the design was first registered, and so changes in taste and fashion can be followed. The table given on page 25 will enable the reader to date all clear marks. The class number appears in a circle at the top of the diamond device.

For several years I have been building up a reference collection of pottery and porcelain bearing the registration mark. This has proved a most interesting study, with the added attraction that specimens can be found in most second-hand or small antique shops and can be purchased at little cost. The collector of registered designs will have many surprises; fine quality porcelains offered for sale as 'Rockingham *c.* 1820' will be found to be produced by early Victorian manufacturers of whom most dealers or collectors have never heard (see Plate 6). The correct date can be readily ascertained from the Table of year and month letters on page 25. The original drawings and manufacturer's name can be traced in the thick Board of Trade files which are still preserved. Many examples, often from little-known manufacturers, can be attributed by reference to the official files. As several of these small firms did not use a factory mark the pieces bearing the registration mark are the only objects that can be attributed to them with certainty.

It is not possible to trace the *name* of the registering firm from any published table or list; the official files contain over five thousand different designs and unless the mark is very plain, it is a very lengthy process to find the one which is the object of the search.

Few collectors can house examples of the thousands of patterns and forms registered in china alone. There are, however, many subdivisions from which specimens can be collected, both for their decorative merits and for the serious study of the wares of a particular district or period. Most collectors will find the period from 1842 to 1852 of greatest interest. This ten-year period saw less than six hundred different ceramic designs registered, for the manufacturers were at first slow to take advantage of the protection that the Act provided; in the first full year (from September 1842 to September 1843) only twenty-six ceramic designs were submitted, while in the 1870s and the 1880s this number was often exceeded each month.

The majority of entries in the files cover printed patterns. Many of these, especially the earlier ones, are most decorative and show a very high standard of engraving. Some really charming landscape designs were produced with gay figures parading about. As any printed design was applied to a variety of shapes,

7. Children's plates by Bailey & Ball of Longton. Moulded border design registered in March 1847. The centres occur with many different printed subjects.

a fine varied collection can be formed. Plates are most often met with but although these show the printed pattern to advantage, few people will want to collect only plates; the search for the rarer pieces – tureens, mugs, bowls, etc., adds much to the pleasure of collecting.

Very many registered designs, then, were concerned solely with the printed pattern, but others were for the moulded decorative border or edge to a plate or dish. One such design registered by the little-known firm of Bailey and Ball of Stafford Street, Longton on 22 March 1847 is shown in Plate 7. This moulded plate design can be found decorated with a variety of typically early Victorian prints: the plates could never have been expensive and were probably originally sold as child's

plates at a very few pence, nevertheless they have a wonderful naïve charm that cannot be matched by the more sophisticated wares.

Just as 20th-century potters seem to produce a never-ending supply of fancy or utilitarian ash-trays, so the Victorian potters seem to have specialized in moulded jugs of ornate forms. The Board of Trade files are packed with jug designs. These give the collector a wide choice: he can collect figure subjects, or the very attractive floral designs. They are all finely moulded and occur in several sizes (most jugs were orignally issued in three or four graduating sizes) and in several different coloured bodies. Of these the matt white 'parian' body is the most common and often the most effective. I have a selection of white jugs displayed in a showcase, the inside of which is painted black. Few ceramic objects can give as much pleasure with so little outlay.

8. A selection of moulded parian body jugs by Copelands; W. Brownfield; Beech & Hancock and S. Alcock & Co. Designs registered between 1847 and 1864.

There are so many of these Victorian moulded jugs available that the collector can afford to be discriminating: he should purchase only examples that are pleasing to him – examples that show sharp relief in the moulding, and examples that are perfect. Having observed these principles he can if inclined relax any self-imposed price rules and purchase, occasionally, a fine or rare piece for a more considerable sum.

Many early moulded jugs will be found to bear Messrs Copeland's impressed name mark; these are invariably of good design and workmanship. Other fine pieces were made by Samuel Alcock & Co. of the Hill Pottery, Burslem or by Mintons of Stoke-on-Trent. After 1851 William Brownfield of Cobridge, in the Staffordshire Potteries, issued a long and interesting series. His examples often display ornate moulded marks incorporating the initials 'W.B.' to which '& S' was added after 1870. In contrast to the many designs issued by the manufacturers mentioned above some short-lived firms issued only one design. A case in point is Messrs Clementson, Young and Jameson of Broad Street, Shelton, Hanley, who registered a design in January 1845; in October of the same year the firm appears under the new style of Clementson & Young. A close study of these official files and other contemporary records underlines the continuous changes that were going on in the Staffordshire Potteries – partnerships were formed and quickly broken up. Typical 'registered' jug forms are illustrated in Plate 8.

Another interesting, instructive and decorative line for collectors of 'Registered Designs' lies in teapots. The change in taste and form from 1842 to 1883 is most marked. Most entries for teapots relate only to the basic form, so that one shape can be found with several different styles of decoration. During the later part of the period many fancy shapes were registered and several were made by obscure manufacturers, not only in Staffordshire but in Scotland.

The collector of the products of several fashionable factories would be well advised to study registered designs, for many factories that did not at this period mark their wares registered their designs. I have many fine examples of Coalport porcelain of the 1842–55 period but they are unmarked except for the diamond shaped device. These specimens would be missed by most collectors. Similarly the wares made by the Grainger factory at Worcester seldom bear a maker's mark but several good pieces can be traced by means of the diamond-shaped mark they bear.

From the 1870s several factories produced and registered small decorative fancy objects, many of which are well worth collecting. It should not be taken for granted that all examples bearing a British Registration mark were made in this country, as several foreign manufacturers and agents registered designs that were to be sold in England.

9. Page from a Sampson Smith catalogue showing typical models, most of which were unmarked.

It must not be thought that all pieces bearing the registration mark can be purchased for a few pounds. Some very fine pieces by the leading firms – Mintons, Royal Worcester, Copelands, Royal Crown Derby, etc. – are justly expensive, but the main value of these official records of designs lies in the fact that the average inexpensive day by day products of the small manufacturers can be dated and their makers identified with certainty. It is these wares which can still be found in sufficient quantity to be inexpensive and as yet neglected. The field is so large that personal taste can play its rightful place in making the collection individual and reflecting the personality of the collector.

These notes have mainly been concerned with designs intended for pottery and porcelain but, as can be seen from the list of classes printed on page 20, nearly every type of ware ranging from furniture to lace was covered by the regulations and may be found bearing the diamond-shaped device. It is one of my ambitions to see a national exhibition of these 1842–83 registered designs staged to show really documentary examples of inexpensive Victorian wares, as opposed to the exhibition tours-de-force which are much publicized and only serve to prejudice our view of Victorian Art.

From January 1884 a new system of marking registered designs was employed. The official entries were numbered consecutively and the relevant number marked on each design; the numbers were usually prefixed with the abbreviation 'Rd No.' The table on page 25 will show the year of registration of designs registered prior to 1909. It must be remembered that with all systems of registration the official mark will show only the date that the design was first introduced and this is not necessarily the date of manufacture.

TABLE OF REGISTRATION MARKS
1843–1883

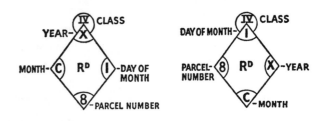

ABOVE ARE the two patterns of Design Registration Marks that were in current use between the years 1842 and 1883. Keys to 'year' and 'month' code-letters are given below.

The left-hand diamond was used during the years 1842 to 1867. A change was made in 1868, when the right-hand diamond was adopted.

10. Page from a pre-war catalogue issued by William Kent of Burslem. This potter produced many figures from 18th and early 19th century moulds.

INDEX TO YEAR AND MONTH LETTERS
YEARS

1842–67
Year Letter at Top

A = 1845	N = 1864	A = 1871	L = 1882
B = 1858	O = 1862	C = 1870	P = 1877
C = 1844	P = 1851	D = 1878	S = 1875
D = 1852	Q = 1866	E = 1881	U = 1874
E = 1855	R = 1861	F = 1873	V = 1876
F = 1847	S = 1849	H = 1869	W = (1–6 Mar.)
G = 1863	T = 1867	I = 1872	1878
H = 1843	U = 1848	J = 1880	X = 1868
I = 1846	V = 1850	K = 1883	Y = 1879
J = 1854	W = 1865		
K = 1857	X = 1842		
L = 1856	Y = 1853		
M = 1859	Z = 1860		

1868–83
Year Letter at Right

MONTHS (BOTH PERIODS)

A = December	G = February	M = June
B = October	H = April	R = August
C or O = January	I = July	(and 1–19
D = September	K = November (and	September
E = May	December 1860)	1857)
		W = March

TABLE OF DESIGN REGISTRATION NUMBERS, FOUND ON WARES FROM 1884

Rd No.	1	registered in January 1884
Rd No.	19754	registered in January 1885
Rd No.	40480	registered in January 1886
Rd No.	64520	registered in January 1887
Rd No.	90483	registered in January 1888
Rd No.	116648	registered in January 1889
Rd No.	141273	registered in January 1890
Rd No.	163767	registered in January 1891
Rd No.	185713	registered in January 1892
Rd No.	205240	registered in January 1893
Rd No.	224720	registered in January 1894
Rd No.	246975	registered in January 1895
Rd No.	268392	registered in January 1896
Rd No.	291241	registered in January 1897
Rd No.	311658	registered in January 1898
Rd No.	331707	registered in January 1899
Rd No.	351202	registered in January 1900
Rd No.	368154	registered in January 1901
Rd No.	385500*	registered in January 1902
Rd No.	402500*	registered in January 1903
Rd No.	420000*	registered in January 1904
Rd No.	447000*	registered in January 1905
Rd No.	471000*	registered in January 1906
Rd No.	494000*	registered in January 1907
Rd No.	519500*	registered in January 1908
Rd No.	550000*	registered in January 1909

Approximate numbers only

11. Staffordshire earthenware Chicken nest egg box of a type made by many manufacturers.

CHAPTER THREE

STAFFORDSHIRE CHIMNEY ORNAMENTS

THE NAME 'Staffordshire' has been given to a large class of decorative earthenware figures produced throughout the 19th century. Most of these were made in the Staffordshire Potteries but many were made outside Staffordshire, by North country and Scottish Potters.

Most perfect examples made before the 1840s are outside the price range covered by this book, but there remains vast scope for the collector in the thousands of charming figures and groups made from the 1840s onwards. Within recent years several fine collections of named Victorian portrait figures have been built up and learned books written on the figures and the characters they portray. The interest in this facet of the subject has caused most of the portrait figures to become expensive, but the purely ornamental figures and groups have been largely neglected and good examples can still be purchased with little trouble for a few pounds. There is ample scope for individual taste and adjustment to the space available.

All these earthenware figures have a simple Victorian charm; they were produced at low cost for cottage ornamentation and many were reputedly sold at local Fairs. The contemporary term for the figures was Toys or Images. Nineteenth-century Directories list many Toy manufacturers but extremely few of these makers troubled to mark their inexpensive wares. Contemporary references to this class of earthenware are likewise very scarce, the most interesting relating to George Hood's Toy Manufactory at Burslem. This was written by an employee, C. Shaw, in the 1840s. The works were probably typical of most small potteries of the period.

'... The toy manufactory itself was a curiosity in structure and management. It was rusty and grim. As for form, it might have been brought in cartloads from the broken down cottages on the opposite side of the street. The workshops were neither square, nor round, nor oblong. They were a jumble of the oddest imaginable kind, and if there had been the ordinary number of workshops on an average sized pot-works, placed as these were placed, it would have been impossible to have found the way in and the way out ... Only about a dozen people were employed on the 'bank', and if we all turned out together we were thronged in the narrow spaces outside the shops.

'I remember the figure of Napoleon Bonaparte was the leading article of our industry at this toy factory ... He had a dark blue coat on, tightly buttoned, a buff waistcoat and white breeches. There were touches of gold on his coat and on his large black hat, with flat sides and point, with a high peak. These Napoleons must have been in large demand somewhere, for shoals of them were made at this time ... We made cats, too, on box-lids, representing cushions. We made dogs of all sizes, from 'Dignity' to 'Impudence'. We made the gentlest of swains and the sweetest of maids, nearly always standing under the shade of a tree ...'

Another rare reference to Staffordshire figure ornaments is contained in *The Leisure Hour*, a family journal of instruction and recreation, published weekly. In the issue of 2 June 1853 under the heading 'A visit to the Staffordshire Potteries' and of Longton in particular, the writer noted:

'An immense quantity of the low-priced English china, as well for exportation as for home consumption is here manufactured weekly, as well as earthenwares of all kinds, and toys consisting of images in gold and colours of men and women, and rustic groups, and dogs and cats, and Swiss cottages, and Bonapartes, Victorias, Great Moguls, Dukes of Wellington, Tom Thumbs, Shepherds, Dairymaids, Cows, John Bulls and John Wesleys, etc., etc., as the advertisements say "too numerous to mention".'

The reader may discover for himself other references, hidden away in Victorian journals or novels. Many interesting facts can be gleaned from the most unlikely sources. I found important references in a book of poems by a Canadian. The booklet, *The Thirteenth Londoniad*, was published by James Torrington Spencer Lidstone, in 1866. This Canadian visited individual Potteries and wrote 'poems' on the potters and the wares he had seen; each is printed under a heading giving the firm's official style and address and a description of the wares produced. I quote brief extracts from two poems in which earthenware figures are mentioned:

WILLIAM STUBBS. Manufacturer of china and earthenware ornaments, metal top jugs, candlesticks, figures, toys, lustre, etc. Eastwood Pottery, Hanley, Staffordshire Potteries.

12. A 'Staffordshire dog' of a type produced by Sampson Smith and several other manufacturers.

... Lo; the Polychrome Parian bespoke much taste and Parian Jugs, etc., in design most chaste. Common China (endless variety), figures of angels, preachers, illustrious coloured persons! ...

(William Stubbs worked the Eastwood Pottery from *c.* 1862–97.)

JANE BEECH (late William Beech). Manufacturer of China, Parian and earthenware Fancy Goods. Old Bell Works, Burslem, Staffordshire.

... All you can mention of Bird or Animal, Jane Beech as b'Fairy Wand doth readily up-call, She doth in her line o'er th' Potteries preside, By her is England and the British Isles supplied.

... I've seen of the Legendary Red Riding Hood, Many representations, but never one so good, While the Fowls for Egg Dishes charm each wond'ring land, As if straight from some mighty Sculptor's hand.

(William Beech worked the Bell Works, Burslem from 1834 – Jane continued to 1873; the works must have produced hundreds and thousands of animals and figures in these forty years.)

James Dudson is the only manufacturer to have shown this type of figure at International Exhibitions in 1851 and 1862. One would therefore expect examples made by this Hanley potter to be above average in quality.

Later in the century Trade advertisements give the names of some manufacturers and the types of ware they produced. Here are some advertisements with brief notes on the potters concerned.

SAMPSON SMITH
CHINA, EARTHENWARE FIGURES, SILVER LUSTRE AND JET MANUFACTURER, LONGTON, STAFFORDSHIRE

... Figures, all kinds and sizes, dogs, white and gold, black and gold, red and white and black and white ...

Sampson Smith's name is that most frequently associated with this class of Victorian earthenware figure. A marked example is preserved in the Victoria and Albert Museum and I have a marked group and a Toby jug, but documentary examples are very rare and he could not have produced all the unmarked examples credited to him. Sampson Smith's name first occurs in records of 1851, and in Slater's Directory of 1853 he is listed as a Toy Manufacturer. Very rare examples bear a moulded mark

S. Smith

Longton. It is very doubtful if the date 1851 relates to the year 1851

of manufacture, it is more likely to record his date of establishment. The marked examples I have seen are decorated with 'Bright Gold', not introduced until the early 1880s. 'Sampson Smith' figures were produced from original moulds by subsequent firms up to recent times. In the summer of 1963 I was offered the original moulds together with the remaining stock of (undecorated) figures. The moulds will presumably be purchased by a manufacturer who will continue to produce Sampson Smith models introduced over one hundred years previously. A page from an early 20th-century catalogue is reproduced (see Plate 9) and the reader may well be able to match the drawings with examples in his own collection.

KENT & PARR
WELLINGTON STREET, BURSLEM

Manufacturers of all kinds of Earthenware Figures and ornaments comprising Centre pieces, Dogs, white and gold, black and white, red and white. Hounds, . . . Poodle Dogs, all in several sizes; Watch stands, Hens and a very large assortment of Gross Figures . . .

This partnership worked from *c.* 1880 to 1894 and the Parr name can be traced back to the earlier part of the 19th century. The

Kent and Parr works were continued after *c.* 1894 by William Kent. His *Pottery Gazette* advertisements read:

WILLIAM KENT, Novelty Works, Wellington Street, Burslem. Specialities ; Old Staffordshire Figures. Special lines in Toby jugs, Spaniel Dogs, Poodles, Hounds . . . Horsemen, Cows, etc., etc.

Similar advertisements continue to 1913 but in 1914 only teapots are mentioned. The production of figures was, however, continued after the First World War and up to the outbreak of the Second War. After the war the old firm of William Kent was re-styled William Kent (Porcelain) Ltd. and they began to produce the figures, etc., again, using the original moulds. Production ceased at the end of 1962. A page from a pre-war Kent catalogue is reproduced in Plate 10 but it should be noted that some examples depicted are copied from early 19th-century models.

Another advertiser was William Machin of Hanley. He is first listed at Percy Street in 1875 and after 1884 at the Dresden Works, George Street, Hanley. Advertisements mention figures and, in this case, the information is substantiated in other works. L. Jewitt's *The Ceramic Art of Great Britain*, first edition of 1878, lists under Hanley, 'Percy Street – William Machin makes ordinary earthenware and common coloured figures.' William Scarratt in his *Old Times in the Potteries* (1906), under the head-

14. The same lithophane lit from the rear, so bringing the picture to life.

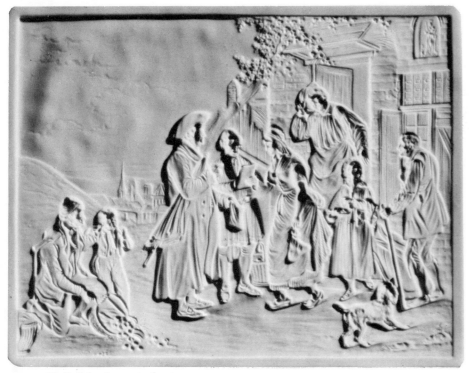

13. Unlit lithophane made at the Plaue Porzellan Manufacktur, Thuringia. Impressed mark P.P.M.

ing 'Figure and Toy Manufactories' – lists former figure makers and then continues 'William Machin, George Street, Hanley. Foreign competition has driven out of this locality nearly all, except the last-named house. The firm still continues, having some rare models.' William Machin continued to 1911.

Pursuing the search of *Pottery Gazette* advertisements we find that of Joseph Unwin (& Co.) in June 1881. The advertisements are simple and read 'JOSEPH UNWIN & Co., Manufacturers of Earthenware figures &c for home and export. Cornhill Works, Longton.' Joseph Unwin started on his own account *c.* 1877 (being formerly in partnership as Poole and Unwin). In 1891 the firm became Joseph Unwin & Co. and as such continued to *c.* 1926. One example has been noted, marked 'Unwin'. I have a similar example – a group of two harvesters with the initial mark of the earlier partnership of Poole and Unwin *c.* 1871–6.

Other *Pottery Gazette* advertisers include J. W. BESWICK of Longton *c.* 1895, continued today as John Beswick Ltd. In the April 1895 issue of *Pottery Gazette*, a writer noted that 'Mr Beswick has an entirely new line of figures of all kinds.' In the following year it was recorded that J. W. Beswick had taken a second works (The Britannia Works in High Street, Longton) owing to increased business. His specialities then included '. . . dogs and figures of all descriptions.' In 1898 his wares included 'dogs, cats and other animals' and an endless variety of figures. It would seem that J. W. Beswick made a great number of late 19th-century Staffordshire figures.

JOHN SADLER of the Central Pottery, Burslem advertised 'Cottage Figures in Great Variety'. A pair of figures of General Sir John French and Lord Kitchener issued about 1900 bear a printed mark SADLER BURSLEM. No other marked examples have apparently been recorded, but this documentary pair enable others in the same series – The Duke of Connaught, Major General Sir Hector Macdonald, General Sir Redvers Buller, Lord Roberts and Colonel Baden-Powell, to be attributed. These portrait figures are probably the last to be specially modelled; most 20th-century examples are re-issues of earlier models. Messrs Lancaster & Sons Ltd of Hanley also made figures early in the present century for a figure has been recorded with the stamped mark LANCASTERS LIMITED, HANLEY, ENGLAND

By the late 1890s the heyday of Staffordshire portrait figures was over. Few new models were produced although the market still absorbed vast quantities of dateless Staffordshire figures and dogs. A writer in the Trade Journal *Pottery Gazette* lamented in 1894–'Where are the English pottery toys? "Big for the money" has killed them – big heroes and big groups for the money have murdered this very lucrative pottery industry, and rightly too!'

This is no doubt true, the simple charm of the earlier figures had given way to commercial cut-price requirements. The figures were simplified and became characterless; size and cheapness were the overriding factors.

The reader having learned that this class of figure was produced from the 1840s up to the present time may well wonder how he is to tell the old specimens from the new. This is difficult to convey in words; it is mainly a question of feel and atmosphere. The Victorian examples give the feeling of being spontaneous productions while the modern reproductions lack life. Often the 20th-century examples are too detailed in the painting and do not show the lively free brushwork of the originals.

The Victorian figures were produced by pressing thin bats of moist clay into a two or three-piece mould. As the bats were worked into the moulds so the fingers left their impressions in the clay; this can clearly be seen in the inside of broken specimens. Most reproductions were produced by pouring liquid clay (termed slip) into the *plaster-of-Paris* mould. After the plaster had absorbed some of the water and formed a clay wall all round the inside of the mould, the surplus liquid was poured away. This method of production leaves a smooth inside to the hollow figure quite unlike the earlier press-moulded examples. On some 20th-century figures the smooth inside can be seen through the large hole that was often left in the base. Victorian figures normally have a closed up base (to hide the unsightly press-moulded interior) with just a very small vent hole to allow the air to escape during the firing process.

In determining the period of Victorian figures one of the main considerations is the general style of the figure or group; often the subject affords the clue to the earliest date of production. Some general rules apply. The earlier figures from about 1840 to 1850 were often of a refined body, very slightly transparent in places. The decoration sometimes included a rich dark underglaze blue, with gilt buttons, etc. This underglaze blue was rarely employed after 1860 as its use necessitated an extra firing and consequent expense in the manufacture. The early figures often have a deeply recessed base, whereas in later examples it is only slightly recessed. The later figures are often noticeably thicker in section and therefore heavier than some of the better quality pre-1850 examples. Figures made after about 1850 normally have flat undecorated backs (hence the term 'flat backs') and a narrow, oval plan indicating that they were intended to stand on a mantelshelf or dresser. Earlier figures are often modelled and decorated back and front and may have a base of circular outline. As the century progressed the models tended to become less complicated so that the figures could be produced at extremely low cost. The gilding employed from the early 1880s is often of a very thin bright nature that did not need burnishing as did the earlier gilding. Once seen this later

"BIJOU TRANSPARENCIES."

THE LATEST NOVELTIES IN ILLUMINATORS.

No. 101.

No. 102.

No. 103.

No. 104.

No. 105.

No. 106.

'bright gold' is easily recognized and is a useful guide to dating.

Other types of Staffordshire ornaments closely linked with these figures are the well-known Staffordshire dogs and hens on nests (see Plates 11 and 12). As can be seen from the advertisements quoted, the dogs were produced by the same potters as the figures.

The standard Staffordshire dog model without a stand or plinth was not made before 1850 (earlier models were on a rocky or other form of base) and the great majority of the dogs were made from the 1880s into the 20th century. For many years I had been searching in mid-Victorian journals, etc., for mention, or a contemporary illustration, of these Staffordshire dogs. One of my most exciting finds was a letter reproduced in the trade paper *Pottery Gazette*.
The letter is dated December 1890 and reads:

Sir,
You would very much oblige me by giving me the names of manufacturers of dog figures made in glazed earthenware

15. *Top*: Lithophane type 'Bijou' novelties as advertised by the British Importers—J. Stembridge & Co in 1888.
16. *Bottom*: Doulton stoneware *c.* 1872–8. The incised animal studies are by Hannah Barlow. The formal leaf pattern jug by Arthur Barlow.

The reply was : 'Our correspondent will be able to obtain these goods from Mr Sampson Smith, Longton and Mr William Machin, Hanley.' This letter not only gave me the name of two manufacturers but it also indicated the late date of many specimens. Examples bearing the moulded mark of Sampson Smith are recorded but are very rare. These dogs are mentioned in the Sampson Smith advertisements quoted earlier in the chapter. Apart from William Machin, other potters who advertised dogs include John Sadler of the Central Pottery, Burslem (1902–32 and continued to the present day as James Sadler & Sons Ltd), and J. W. Beswick of the Gold Street Works, Longton who advertised 'Figures and Dogs of all descriptions'. The firm's successors, John Beswick Ltd today produce these dogs from the original moulds; the modern examples are marked 'BESWICK, ENGLAND'.

Another large producer of the Staffordshire dogs has been William Kent of Burslem (under various styles). An advertisement of the early 1880s lists 'Dogs, White and Gold, Black and White, Red and White ...' The latest illustrated post-war catalogue includes these dogs in eight sizes ranging from 15 inches to 7¼ inches high. The wholesale price in 1939 was 20s. per dozen or 1s. 8d. each!

I have in my collection a pair of dogs bearing the printed trade mark of Lancaster & Sons Ltd of Hanley (c. 1899 onwards). These, like other early 20th-century examples have glass eyes inserted, a feature which will not be found on Victorian examples. I have recently purchased new examples by Arthur Wood & Son (Longport) Ltd. These have the moulded name 'Wood' on the base, and the words 'Made in England'. One of the pair also bears the printed Globe trade mark with the name 'Arthur Wood' on a ribbon. The 20th-century examples are produced by pouring the liquid clay into *plaster-of-Paris* moulds. The remarks printed on page 23 relating to methods of manufacture, apply equally to dogs. The Scottish firm of Charles M. McNay & Sons of the Bridgeness Pottery,

Bo'ness, produced many dog and cat ornaments early in the present century.

A decorative and useful form of mid-Victorian earthenware dish takes the form of a chicken seated on a deep oval nest (see Plate 11). These are in two pieces and the chicken cover lifts off. The articles were, and still are, extremely popular and were made in England, France and Germany. In England they were made by the same 'Toy Manufacturers' that produced the figures. The 1866 poem relating to Jane Beech of Burslem quoted on page 19 mentions:

While the Fowls for Egg Dishes charm each wond'ring land, as if straight from some mightly sculptor's hand.

These dishes have been re-issued in recent years but lack the simple grace of the originals. The Victorian examples often show the normal signs – slight chips, etc., of day to day use, for they were not intended to be cabinet pieces; they were made for use and ornament combined. Other bird or animal form dishes may occasionally be found and add interest to a collection. Most examples are unmarked, but I have a hen on egg nest with the impressed mark 'Dudson'. This potter is also known to have made figures.

A showcase of representative specimens of Staffordshire figures has recently been put on display in Room 137 at the Victoria and Albert Museum, this illustrates the growing interest in these Victorian figures.

Reference Books
VICTORIAN STAFFORDSHIRE PORTRAIT FIGURES. B. Latham. 1953.
STAFFORDSHIRE CHIMNEY ORNAMENTS. R. Haggar. 1955.
STAFFORDSHIRE PORTRAIT FIGURES OF THE VICTORIAN AGE. T. Balston. 1958.
COLLECTING STAFFORDSHIRE POTTERY. L. T. Stanley. 1963.

CHAPTER FOUR

LITHOPHANES OR 'BERLIN TRANSPARENCIES'

SEVERAL ATTEMPTS have been made to describe and define these attractive and inexpensive 19th-century ceramic pictures which may still be found in reasonable numbers. The earliest description is still probably the best and was given by Joseph Marryat over one hundred years ago in his – *A History of Pottery and Porcelain, Medieval and Modern* (1850):

LITHOPHANIE. TABLEAUX LITHOPHANIQUES (Fr.)
Porcelain tablets cast in a mould from a model made in wax, which against the light have the appearance of being painted in grisaille, the various thicknesses of the tablet being so arranged as to give the effects of light and shade. These tablets are made in great perfection at the Royal Manufactories of Berlin and Sèvres. They were invented in 1827 by M. P. de Bourgoing.

The Lithophanic process was patented in England by Robert Griffith Jones on 13 March 1828, having been communicated to him 'by a certain Foreign resident abroad', probably by M. de Bourgoing of Paris, mentioned above. The patent is very interesting as it gives the method of preparing the design and mould from which these tablets were made in quantity.

After the usual preamble and description of the finished object the Patent shows how the Lithophane mould was made:

As to the means of executing such ornamental designs or shadowed drawings upon china and other compositions, a suitable model must first be made in plastic wax, which is spread out in a layer upon the surface of a plate of glass, the substance of the wax being previously prepared or tinted in a suitable manner to give it such degree of opacity or transparency as will in some degree correspond with that of the china or other composition which is to be ornamented, and also the thickness of the layer of wax which is poured out in a melted state upon the surface of the glass must be regulated according to the degree of light that it is capable of transmitting through its substance. Upon the surface of the wax so prepared the artist must proceed according to the means usually practised for modelling wax, to cut away and reduce the thickness of the layer of wax at all those parts which are required to exhibit the light parts of the picture or design, leaving the other parts which are to exhibit the shadows of the full thickness of the wax, and even adding wax in particular places to give an extra thickness where necessary to attain the effect of the deepest shadows; and occasionally for particular objects which are to be exhibited with very defined shadows, they may be cut out as profiles and forms in paper or in pasteboard, or in wood, metal, or other suitable substance, and stuck upon the surface of the wax, the surfaces of such objects being carved in relief to give them different thicknesses in different parts. Or when defined objects as aforesaid are to be represented by lights instead of shadows, suitable profiles or forms cut out as aforesaid in pasteboard, wood, metal, or other suitable substance may be pressed upon and imprinted into the surface of the wax and then withdrawn, so as to leave hollow cavities in the wax in order to reduce the thickness thereof, as the nature of the design requires. In thus modelling for lithophanic china the artist must use discretion and ingenuity for the attainment of the required effect of the particular subject or design he undertakes, and no precise rules or directions can be given; he must employ the various means above stated with judgement, and as he may find them best adapted to obtain the representation of the different effects of light and shade required in the various parts of the piece. The projections and excavations upon the various parts of the surface of lithophanic china are not (as in the case of common embossing and modelling in relief) carved according to the real forms of the subject, but are intended to adapt the degree of thickness of the china at every part according to the intensity of light and of shadow which is requisite to represent the subject, and hence a lithophanic model or

Mid nineteenth-century British earthenwares bearing colored-over printed designs. See Chapter 1.

Selection of Staffordshire earthenware figures or "chimney ornaments" c. 1845-65. See Chapter 3.

Selection of multi-color printed earthenwares by F.&R. Pratt, including typical "pot lids" and related objects c. 1850-70. See Chapter 6.

Selection of German porcelain groups by Conta & Boehme. See Chapter 7.

lithophanic china, when viewed upon an opaque ground, presents an irregular, indistinct, and unfinished surface, with very little of the effect of the design, for, like transparent paintings, the lithophanic china must be viewed against the light to exhibit the light and shadow of a picture. Hence during the process of modelling the design in wax as aforesaid, the model must be frequently held up to the light to examine the progress and effect of the work and to govern the modelling accordingly. The model in wax or original design being prepared by a judicious application of the various means above described, and of all other suitable means usually practised in modelling in wax, a cast or mould must be taken from the model in plaster, which mould will consequently be in reverse to the model; then from such mould the required number of casts or copies may be obtained in china, in the manner commonly practised for taking casts of ornamental figures in china. If it is desired to produce a very finished and delicate design with a strong effect of light and shade, the first plaster cast or mould which is taken from the wax model, and in reverse thereto, may be retouched by carving and cutting away at all those parts which are required to exhibit very deep and defined shadows and dark outlines, such as would have been difficult to execute with sufficient relief and sharpness on the surface of the wax model. For instance, the naked branches of trees, railings, the outlines of buildings, figures, and similar objects, which must be represented by dark lines, should be carved out in the hollow parts of the first mould. From that first mould when so prepared a cast should be taken either in plaster or in china, which will be a counterpart of the original model, but more perfect and in higher relief at all the shadowed parts and dark outlines. That cast should be again retouched, in order to cut away and reduce the thin parts where requisite, to improve the parts which are to exhibit the lights, by carving or graving the surface to reduce the thickness of those parts. Lastly, a metal mould of pewter, tin or type metal, or brass, or other suitable metal, should be taken from the said cast, and the finishing touches for the sharp outlines and deep shadows may be engraved in the hollows of that metal mould. For instance, to attain the effect for the more delicate strokes of the design, such as the lineaments of the face, the hands, the embroidery of garments, suitable finishing touches must be put in with the graver. These operations of retouching upon the hollow moulds and the metal required even more skill and attention than the first operation of modelling in wax, because the artist can only judge of his work by his previous knowledge of the effect it will produce. In order to guide him as to the depth of cut he is to make with his graver, the impressions or casts for highly finished lithophanic china are taken from the last metal mould when prepared as above described, and such impressions and casts are to be burned and treated in every respect in the same manner as ornamental figures in china or biscuit are usually treated, and the surface of the lithophanic china may be further ornamented in colours, and glazed if thought desirable . . .

Jones' Patent was probably sold to Messrs Grainger, Lee & Co. of Worcester. Their examples are very rare but some attractive night light containers incorporate lithophane type panels which were brought to life by a night light. A mould for a Grainger lithophane is still preserved and shows a standing woman before her dressing-table. The lithophane process seems to have been sadly neglected in England until the early 1850s although the Berlin factory in Germany was manufacturing large numbers of lithophanic panels before this period. It is because of the popularity of the imported Berlin pieces that the English potters later sought to produce examples in England.

An invoice dated February 1850, discovered at Mintons, refers to 'Berlin Transparencies'; these were probably purchased in Berlin for Mintons to copy, but examples had been made at Mintons before this date for a letter written in January

17. Earthenware jug and pot lid both bearing multi-coloured prints by Liddle, Elliot & Son. The jug form was registered in 1863.

1848 refers to them. The prices given against each subject are 'Berlin Prices' which presumably means the cost to the purchaser in Berlin. The list of 1850 examples with prices reads:

The Penitent	12/–	Guardian Angel	11/6
Naomi and her daughters-in-law	10/–	Quentin Durward	7/6
		Mother and Dying Child	7/6
The Merry Musician	7/6	The Agony in the Garden	
The Merry Story Teller	7/6		3/6
Mother and children	9/–	The Jolly Good Fellow	3/6
The Offering	7/6		

Mintons produced Lithophane panels and some of the original open moulds have been found at the factory. When, as an experiment, some few panels were recently produced from these moulds, difficulty was experienced in firing the very thin tablets as they tended to warp in the kiln. One of these modern trials was kindly given to me and shows a Church or Cathedral in an open square. I do not know of any marked examples of Minton's lithophanic panels, but the moulds discovered at the factory include a mountain view, a cow with calf by a pond, a woman kneeling before an altar and the cathedral in a square.

Examples were also made at the South Wales Pottery at Llanelly. A report in *The Cambrian Journal*, Vol. 1, 1854 lists various types of ware produced and mentions that: '. . . transparent tableaux of imitation Parian and beautifully executed, and perfected at a trifling cost.' An example in the National Museum of Wales, at Cardiff, depicts a vine branch and grapes. This is impressed marked 'South Wales Pottery'; other examples may bear the initials 'S.W.P.' At this period, 1854–8, the South Wales Pottery was managed by Coombs & Holland, and subsequently by Holland and Guest.

Other British firms to manufacture lithophanes include Cope-

18. Doulton stoneware modelled
    by George Tinworth and
    bearing his incised G.T.
    monogram. Group 5½″ high.

land, W.H.Goss and Wedgwood; the latter firm produced small lithophanic shades for night lights, etc. The Belleek factory in Ireland also made lithophanic panels; the practice was reputedly introduced by Ross, the foreman from the South Wales Pottery. An example has been reported with the impressed mark 'BELLEEK, FERMANAGH'. Some of the better English examples have been tinted, a process which no doubt increased the price but which resulted in a charming effect. The suggestion was included in Jones' Patent of 1828. Some writers have stated that Kennedy, Adderley & Lawson made lithophanes but I have been unable to trace the existence of these potters!

Some reference books have stated that the Kennedy Porcelain Manufactory, Burslem produced marked examples. No English firm of this name is recorded, and one can only presume that an effort has been made to invent a firm to match the initials 'K.P.M.' found on many lithophanes of German make.

By far the greatest proportion of lithophanic china was manufactured on the Continent. As we have seen the process was invented there, and in a book published in 1850 the tablets of the Royal Manufactory of Berlin are especially mentioned. In the official catalogue of the 1851 Exhibition held in Hyde Park 'The Royal Prussian Porcelain Manufactory' exhibited 'Lithophanies'. The mark used by this State factory at this period was the initials 'K.P.M.' and many lithophanic panels may be found with these impressed initials, followed by a number, which related to the factory list or catalogue. Later in the century other Continental firms used the initials.

At this period decorative wares other than panels were made. At the Great Exhibition of 1851, Diedr Meyer of Hamburg showed a 'night lamp with two lithophanic plates'. Later in the 19th century many novelties were introduced incorporating lithophanic panels. The advertisement of 1888 reproduced in plate 15 shows typical Continental examples.

The Meissen or Dresden factory also made lithophanic wares. The official 1910 commemorative book states; 'In 1828 the Lithophanien or lamp – shades of quite thin transparent china were introduced ... and were exceedingly popular.' At the 1851 Exhibition the Dresden Works exhibited 'Shades' which may well have been of the lithophanic type.

The Royal Copenhagen Manufactory in Denmark made lithophane panels in the late 1840s and early 1850s. Factory records prove that at least two subjects were produced – the sculptor Thorvaldsen at work and a profile portrait of King Frederick VII, but these do not seem to have been marked.

Many of the finest lithophane panels bear the impressed initials 'P.P.M.'; these were probably made at the Plaue Porzellan Manufaktur at Plaue-on-Havel, Thuringia – a good example is reproduced in Plates 13 and 14. Other examples are marked 'B.P.M.' (Buckau Porzellan Manufaktur, Magdeburg). Examples made at Henneberg's factory at Gotha, are sometimes impressed in full 'Hennebergsche Porzellan Manufaktur' or with the initials 'H.P.M.'. The Klasterec factory in Bohemia produced under Karl Venier's management (1848), 'Lithophane or diaphane shades with figure compositions. They represented various genre themes, mythological statues [sic], historical scenes from Napoleonic times, ladies in period costume, reproductions of picture supplements in current fashion books and so on.' (English translation of Emmanual Pocock's *Bohemian Porcelain*.) The mark employed by the Klasterec factory at this period was the impressed initials 'T.K.'. Other Bohemian lithophanes were made at Schlaggenwald.

Many French examples of panels, lampshades and novelties bear marks incorporating the initials 'P.R.' sometimes with a sickle-like trade mark. Several are marked 'Lithophanie Francaise' and some are of extremely fine quality.

The simple panels can still be found at low cost; the night light shapes and other novelties are difficult to find and unless one is very lucky, will be beyond the basic five pound price range covered by this book. Nevertheless, these rarities should be purchased as opportunity permits.

The novelties were originally lit by means of night lights or candles (see Plate 15). It is difficult to arrange this in a cabinet but low powered bulbs can be affixed instead. A selection of illuminated lithophane novelties in a special display case, perhaps with the background and shelves painted black, can be very striking. The panels could be displayed in a case with a false back into which these panels are inset. Behind the false back a source of light is permitted. If electric or other artificial means of lighting are arranged ample ventilation must be made. Many other decorative uses can be found for lithophanic panels; they would be specially effective inset into doors, so that the light from a hall or room illuminates the panel which can be seen from the outside or dark side.

CHAPTER FIVE

DOULTON STONEWARES AND
FAIENCE

To THE COLLECTOR seeking an inexpensive but interesting field the various Doulton wares, made at Lambeth, offer wide scope. Prior to 1870 Doultons may be said to have specialized in purely utilitarian and industrial pottery although some decorative flasks, etc., had been made from the 1830s.

Their new Art Pottery was included in and acclaimed at the South Kensington Exhibition of 1871 (early experimental pieces were included in the Paris Exhibition of 1867 but these were not a complete success); from 1871 onwards the decorative side of the firm went from strength to strength. From an early date the collectors' requirements were kept in mind and the individual character of the works underlined. The *Art Journal* magazine recorded in 1872 – 'it is not their intention to produce them in sets or to make duplicates, in order that the unique character of these products may be sustained; having in perspective the time when such wares may be sought for and gathered into collections and museums'.

The Doulton Stonewares made at Lambeth are of a fine, highly fired, salt glazed stoneware; the early pieces have a simple charm that is sometimes lacking in later examples. Most Doulton wares are signed by the artist who decorated them; all bear one or other form of factory mark and most pieces bear the date of production. The discriminating collector can today form an interesting and decorative collection at little cost. The amount of Doulton ware produced and still available is very large and the collector would be well advised to restrict his attention to the earlier examples made before 1885, or to the work of one of the many artists who decorated by hand the individual designs.

Henry Doulton was probably the first potter to employ female labour on a large scale to decorate his wares with individual designs; many of the artists were students from the government schools of design that were beginning to appear. The trouble was that, once trained, they could not be placed in industry to use their newly acquired talents. The success of Henry Doulton's experiment did much to ensure that other manufacturers sought to employ the female students. As we shall see, these Doulton students were permitted to practice their own individual styles, and many of them quickly acquired a national and sometimes international reputation.

Early contemporary accounts of Doultons' new art wares are to be found in the monthly magazine – the *Art Journal*. The issue of January 1872 is interesting as it relates to wares shown at the 1871 Exhibition. The report reads in part:

'The specimens exhibited (by Doultons) in the pottery gallery were selected from a small number made specially to illustrate the application of ornament of a simple character to ordinary stoneware. It was not then intended to carry this class of manufacture further, but the result of the idea was such as no active firm could, for many reasons, afford to overlook. These examples were received with so much satisfaction, and commented on so favourably by persons of known taste and learning in such matters, that the firm, consulting their own interests and reputation, determined to continue the manufacture of these products in so far as they should find favour with the public.

'Messrs Doultons have undoubtedly employed artists extensively; but now we understand that to their establishment have been attached artists educated at the Lambeth School of Art – a measure which must be adopted by all producers of articles in terra-cotta and stoneware . . .

'The objects produced by Messrs Doulton include many beautiful forms that have descended to us from antiquity. Some of the upright forms with plain cups and lips, and resting on florid or Melon-shaped bases, are of elegant proportions . . . We are never weary of contemplating them and return to them with increasing admiration after considering the abuses of proportion and vulgarity of ornament induced by desire of novelty.

'The ornament is principally the Sgraffimento [generally called 'Sgraffiato] or incised outline, which is effected sometimes as soon as the vessel leaves the wheel, or more generally after it has been allowed partially to dry to a consistency which will allow of its being handled though yet sufficiently soft to admit of being easily worked upon. The designs are various and are tastefully adapted to the style of the vessel or object; for instance, on the occasion of our visit to these works, the artist was working on a small vase of Pompeian shape, around which were drawn laurel leaves reaching to the neck of the vase, this was held in the left hand while the draughtsman operated on the surface by marking the outline with a stile, following the lines of a pencil sketch; thus this process, although conducted with the utmost precision, is comparatively rapid . . . To the ornament thus engraved in outline, especially to the leafage, colour is applied with an ordinary water-colour brush, and so burnt in . . . Prominent in this throng of novelties are claret cups, loving cups, hot and cold water jugs, flower vases, candlesticks, hunting jugs, pitchers and ink-stands, with a great variety of other vessels and utensils which may be appointed to a multitude of uses . . .'

The quotation is one of the first relating to Doultons' newly introduced decorative, as opposed to utilitarian, stoneware. The remainder of this book could be devoted to later reviews of their wares, often written in the most glowing terms, but I will leave the collector to have the excitement of discovering these for himself and gleaning from them interesting notes on individual artists, etc. The *Art Journal* and *Magazine of Art* will afford much information and copies can be found in most large, public libraries.

I am continually amazed by the amount of documentary evidence that is still available to the inquiring collector of Victorian objects, if he or she will only take the trouble to seek it. The collector of Doulton ware is particularly fortunate in that there is preserved in the Lambeth Public Library (Minet Branch Library, London, S.E.5) two unique volumes presented to Henry Doulton in 1881 by his artists. These books record the name of each artist, and his or her position and department; against the names are the initials monograms or other signs that the artists used on wares which they decorated. The other volume contains a photograph of each artist. The first presentation book has the following address:

Dear Sir, Ten years having now elapsed since the introduction of female employment into the Lambeth Art Pottery we, the undersigned, being the whole of the Lady Artists and Assistants now engaged in the Studios upon the work, desire to take this opportunity of expressing our obligation to you for the origination of an occupation at once interesting and elevating to so large a number of our sex. We also desire to record our very high appreciation of the arrangements made for our comfort and convenience in the various sections.

Each year since the opening of the Art Studio has seen a large increase in our numbers and an extension of the variety of decoration. There has also been an extended patronage and appreciation on the part of art critics and the public while the continued demand for our productions leads us to the conviction that we are fully justified in congratulating you on the marked success of the undertaking. . . . . Yours most faithfully.

This book also records that the number of female artists rose from 1 in 1872 to 231 in December 1881.

Most examples of Doulton stonewares will be found to bear the initials of the decorating artist. The following notes relate to some of the more important of them; their individual monograms, and the various Doulton trade marks will be found in my *Encyclopaedia of British Pottery and Porcelain Marks* (1964).

HANNAH B. BARLOW (1851–1916) was the first female artist to be employed at Doultons after training at the Lambeth School of Art. She became internationally famous for her spirited incised 'drawings' of animal subjects (see Plate 16). These are incised into the soft clay body before firing; the lines are then accentuated with pigment, the strength of the colour depending on the depth of the incised line and the amount of colour it will hold. The object was then fired and salt glazed in the normal manner. All Hannah Barlow's animal studies were drawn freehand and each is unique. All her work bears the 'B.H.B.' monogram on the base of the ware, with Doulton's mark and often the date. Miss Barlow's right hand became partially paralysed, probably through daily contact with the damp, cold clay, but she mastered this disability and learned to draw with equal effect with her left hand until her retirement in 1906. The earlier simple designs are particularly recommended to collectors. After about 1895 the designs tended to become more detailed and fussy, with heavy borders that detract from the overall design rather than enhance it. Probably the best general summary of Hannah Barlow's art occurs in an American book – *Salt Glazed Stoneware*, written by E.A. Barber in 1907:

Among the best artists in this line of work is Miss Hannah B. Barlow, whose etchings of animals were first seen in this country at the Philadelphia Centennial Exhibition in 1876. Since then her work has become familiar to all lovers of art on this side of the Atlantic.

Her spirited renderings of horses, dogs, sheep and rustic life, in the fewest possible lines, are truly remarkable, and she has been placed by competent critics next to Rosa Bonheur as a delineator of animal life.

FLORENCE E. BARLOW at first worked in a similar technique to her sister, Hannah, but Florence specialized in incised studies of birds. Later she developed a charming style in which the birds, foliage, etc., are built up in low relief in coloured clays. Florence Barlow joined Doultons in 1873; she died in 1909. Her work is signed with various monograms of the initials 'F.B.' or 'F.E.B.'.

ARTHUR B. BARLOW. This artist, brother of Hannah and Florence, produced some very good incised and modelled formal floral patterns on early Doulton stonewares, from 1872 until his early death in February 1879. His designs are always well suited to the object and I have never seen a fussy example of his work (see Plate 16). His work bears the incised monogram 'A.B.B.'.

JOHN BROAD was a very talented figure modeller employed from the early 1870s until his death in 1919. He exhibited at several Royal Academy Exhibitions, and the collector will be extremely fortunate to find his work in the price range covered by this book. His sculpture is signed with the joined initials 'J.B.'.

FRANK A. BUTLER joined Doultons in 1873. He was both deaf and dumb and had little interest in life outside his work at Doultons; he lived his life in his art. Frank Butler's rapid, bold carved and modelled designs soon won high praise, Mr Gladstone being one of the admirers of his work. In 1877, a specimen was purchased for the Victoria and Albert Museum. He retired in 1911, having designed and finished thousands of individual patterns for Doultons. His incised mark is made up of the initials 'F.A.B.'.

EMILY J. EDWARDS was an early Doulton artist, joining the staff in 1872; her work is rare for she died early in 1879. Her work is made up of elaborate stamped patterns, often of a formal floral nature; her monogram mark is made up of the initials 'E.J.E.'.

LOUISA E. EDWARDS worked from about 1873 to 1890. Her patterns are reminiscent of Indian or Persian floral patterns but have a style that was entirely her own.

FRANCES E. LEE was employed during the 1875–90 period; her work combined pressed and incised motifs of a formal nature. Her mark comprises the initials 'F.E.L.'.

EDITH D. LUPTON worked from c. 1876 to 1889. Her work is typical of the Doulton commercial floral patterns of the period. Her initials 'E.D.L.' will be found on specimens.

MARK V. MARSHALL. This potter, designer and sculptor received early training with the Martin Brothers (the first of the Studio Potters). He joined Doultons in 1876 and stayed with them until his death in 1912. His work is often on a large scale and such important specimens will command a high price; he did, however, make some small pieces. J. F. Blacker wrote in 1922 of a 9-inch vase: 'It is of a perfect pear-shape-inverted form, with a salamander, in relief and open-work, clinging round the neck and body on a background of low relief foliage like giant seaweed, exquisitely finished, a marvel of colouring, a proof of the capacity of salt glaze for colour schemes without a jarring tone – greys and blues, purples and greens with the animal spotted with the nearest approach to peach bloom possible . . .' The initials 'M.V.M.' will be found on Mark V. Marshall's work.

MARY MITCHELL specialized in incised drawings of figures – mostly children in landscapes. Her work is comparable with Hannah Barlow's animal studies, but is much rarer. Her working period was 1876–87 and the distinguishing mark the initials 'M.M.'.

ELIZA SIMMANCE was a very prolific artist who was employed at Doultons from c. 1873 to 1928. Her work is mainly floral in character, finely incised, carved, moulded in relief and coloured. Her mark was a large 'S' with a small 'e' in the centre.

GEORGE TINWORTH. This modeller is justly the most famous of all Doulton artists. He is chiefly known for his finely modelled terra-cotta plaques of religious subjects which may be seen in many churches and chapels. They enjoyed wide publicity at the time and today examples seldom come on the market – they are certainly outside the scope of the present book. But George Tinworth is also famous for a series of comical animal groups engaged in human pursuits (see Plate 18). They show him to be a talented modeller with a gay sense of fun, but, here again, the collector will be very fortunate to purchase specimens at under five pounds.

As a change from the time-absorbing religious plaques and other monumental work that Tinworth was commissioned to do, he carved more ordinary pieces. To use his own words:

'It is a change to go from one subject to another; I cannot finish off a piece satisfactorily with a tired mind. Turn to something else and I come back to the first with powers refreshed . . . one day a week, I etch scrolls and decorations on vases . . . every touch must be true at once, there must be no rubbing out of the lines on the vase when once made.'

These 'one-day-a-week' vases offer the collector a chance to find

Tinworth-decorated Doulton at under five pounds. Like other pieces from this master hand, they bear the incised monogram made up of the initials 'T.G.'.

George Tinworth joined Doultons in 1867 and continued with them until his death in 1917; his work did much to popularize Doultons' decorative wares throughout the world. The contemporary description of him as 'that Rembrandt in clay' was not wholly unwarranted and the collector would be well advised to remember his name and mark. A diary kept by Mrs. Tinworth in 1888 has recently been discovered, there are several references to plaques and animal models made in that year.

Doulton stonewares offer a wonderful opportunity for the small budget collector. J. F. Blacker's *The A.B.C. of English Salt-Glaze Stone-Ware* (1922) will be found an indispensable reference book.

All these artists decorated Doultons' *stonewares* – a very hard clay-coloured body, but many Doulton wares will be found in an off-white earthenware body, termed 'Doulton Faience'; the name Faience occurs as part of the mark on such wares. This earthenware body was not carved, incised or modelled, as was the stoneware, but painted in the normal way.

The Faience body was introduced about 1873 and a large number of female free-hand artists were employed in decorating the ware, normally vases, dishes and plaques, but also tiles. The monograms of the leading decorators are included in my *Encyclopaedia of British Pottery and Porcelain Marks* and information on several of the artists will be found in J. F. Blacker's *The A.B.C. of 19th century English Ceramic Art* (undated but published about 1911).

An early reference to this new body is contained in an article in the *Art Journal* of March 1874, written by Professor Archer, President of the Royal Scottish Society of Arts. Numerous references to Doultons' Faience ware will be found in Victorian art magazines. An interesting contemporary account by a ceramic student in 1876, records his views on a visit to Howell and James, Regent Street Galleries, prompted by the following advertisement:

LAMBETH FAIENCE – The new art Pottery – The Second Annual Exhibition of orginal Works of Decorative Art in Lambeth. Faience by the students of the Lambeth School of Art is now on view at Messrs Howell and James Art Pottery Galleries, 5, 7, 9, Regent Street, Pall Mall, London. Connoisseurs are invited to visit the Exhibition which contains the finest examples of this highly prized ware that have been produced.

The anonymous student reported:

'I mounted a few steps and found myself in the presence of Doulton's Lambeth Faience and Stoneware. The general effect of the gallery exceeded my expectations, and there were so many nice things to look at, I found it puzzling to know what to purchase. The Doulton Faience is slightly coarse in appearance, with flat looking designs on it, generally of flowers and foliage. The colour is for the most part sober and soft in tone, tertiary shades being much used. The shape of the vases, etc., was good, and the designs and colouring broad in effect ... The whole exhibition does great credit to the Doulton factory, and to the students from the Lambeth School of Art (principally young ladies, I am told) who design for it. This new industry struck me as being of great artistic merit, and an almost entire absence of the crockery-shop style of design and very noticeable ...'

The production of the Doulton Faience ware ceased about 1914.

The Doulton Stoneware and Faience mentioned in this chapter were made and decorated at Lambeth in London. In 1882 Messrs Doultons took over Pinder, Bourne & Co.'s factory in Nile Street, Burslem, in which they had an interest from 1877. The works were remodelled and enlarged and, in 1884, the production of porcelain was added to that of earthenware. These Burslem wares are of fine quality and won international fame. The marks used are often similar to those used at Lambeth, but the name 'Burslem' replaces 'Lambeth'.

Mr Desmond Eyles' new book *Royal Doulton 1815–1965* is a full detailed official history of the firm, its products and artists.

CHAPTER SIX

POT LIDS

China collectors are now giving good prices for old bear's grease pots, on account of the many beautifully designed ceramic pictures on the covers of these formerly popular 'patch boxes'. POTTERY GAZETTE, 1897.

THE SMALL CIRCULAR earthenware pot lids, variously decorated with multi-coloured prints applied under the glaze, have been collected on a large scale for over sixty years and examples must have been seen by most readers. Detailed reference books, or rather illustrated catalogues of known subjects, have been published in several editions from 1924 to 1960. These books – *Colour Pictures on Pot Lids*, 1924 and 1927; *The Pot Lid Book*, 1931; *The Centenary Pot Lid Book*, 1949; *The Pictorial Pot Lid Book*, 1955 and 1960, are all by one author, the late Harold George Clarke, C.B.E. All past and present collectors are indebted to him for his painstaking research.

The name by which these pot lids are generally known is 'Pratt' after the firm of F. & R. Pratt, of Fenton in the Staffordshire Potteries. Messrs Pratt undoubtedly made most, but not all, examples. In the 1830s and 1840s very many different types of ceramic covered boxes were being produced and decorated by hand painting or with the then normal one colour printed patterns. In 1846 Charles Ford, of Shelton, took out a patent relating to the manufacture of 'small pots or boxes, known among potters as patch boxes, pomatum salve pots . . .'

The fact that in 1847 two further patents were taken out for improved methods of manufacturing these boxes indicates that there was a good and growing trade in such articles. The first 1847 patent is dated 21 October and is in the name of John Ridgway, of Cauldon Place, Staffordshire; it was for 'certain improvements in the manufacture of paste boxes, and other similar articles in china or earthenware, or other plastic materials'. The method of production was for various moulds, profiles or dies to be used in conjunction with the traditional potter's wheel. Another method mentioned in the same patent relates to boxes formed by the clay being pressed in moulds; this was used where shapes other than circular were required. I do not know of any marked examples of John Ridgway's 'paste boxes'.

The second relevant 1847 patent was taken out by Felix Edwards Pratt of F. & R. Pratt & Co. in December 1847 and applied 'to that class of articles which are cylindrical or nearly so on their outer surface, and are formed on the throw wheel, or jigger'. By means of a new 'double gauge' which facilitated rapid and trouble free production, the pots could be accurately formed in a minimum of time. Some authorities have stated that the patent was for the multi-coloured printing process of decoration; this is not so; the Pratt patent refers only to the method of forming the undecorated blanks.

Six weeks later a system of transferring printed subjects in two or more colours on china was taken out in the names of F. W. M. Collins and A. Reynolds. The various methods employed were rather complicated but the pattern was to be introduced to the ware by means of special transfer paper. A second method allowed for each colour to be picked up from separate engraved blocks – 'one for each different colour'. The patent continues: 'The three colours blue, red and yellow, yet wet, are transferred by pressing the paper on to the biscuit (unglazed ware) and when the colours are dried on the ware, damp and remove the transfer paper . . .' Harold Clarke has stated that the Pratt-type pot lids were built up from four

19. Selection of colour printed earthenwares by F. and R. Pratt of Fenton. *Godden of Worthing Ltd.*

20. Pratt type multi-colour printed pot lids by Messrs T. J. and J.
Mayer and succeeding firms at the Dale Hall Works, Burslem.

separate engraved copper plates, three for the different colours and one for the main detail and outline printed in brown or black. Great skill and experience was required to line up, or register, each succeeding sheet of transfer paper to give a clear, unblurred picture. Small circles or dots found at each side of most pot lid pictures were used to facilitate the accurate positioning of each succeeding print.

At the 1851 Exhibition, Messrs F. & R. Pratt exhibited 'a variety of box covers, and a pair of ornamental vases in the same style'. The official catalogue then notes that 'these subjects are executed under the glaze by the ordinary process of bisque printing, each colour is produced from a separate engraving and the transfer requires to be carefully registered'. The Jury's report on these exhibits noted that F. & R. Pratt & Co. 'exhibit some very remarkable specimens of a process which they seem to have greatly improved, viz. that of colour printing under the glaze. The freshness and truth of the colouring, in some of these specimens, from pictures by Mulready, Wilkie, &c., are excellent.' The Jury awarded Pratts a prize medal for their display. Clarke states that the pot lids exhibited at the 1851 Exhibition were enhanced by the addition of gold; 'the pot lids themselves will be found with an additional quarter-inch gold outer border and in some cases details of the print are heightened with gold'. Some 1851 exhibition wares, however, do not bear this additional decoration and others found with it are too late in period to have been shown in this exhibition.

Before leaving the subject of Pratts' stand at the 1851 Exhibition, it must be stated that this firm also showed other, more

21. Multi-colour printed pot lids with designs registered by Messrs
Bates, Elliot & Co of Burslem between 1870 and 1874.

ornate, wares decorated by the same multi-coloured printing process. These include a fine bread platter with scripture subject – *Christ in the Cornfield*, after an original painting by H. Warren. An example of this is in my own collection; it is signed by Pratt's engraver, Jesse Austin, and is dated in the design 1851. It furthermore bears a rare circular printed mark which includes the wording 'F. & R. Pratt & Co., Fenton. Manufacturers to H.R.H. Prince Albert' arranged around a crown; this mark rarely occurs on other Pratt wares prior to December 1861. Other Pratt exhibits comprised 'two pictures printed in colours, underglaze in earthenware frames' (a fine example can be seen in the Victoria and Albert Museum) and dessert ware printed with the following subjects – *The Last In*, after Mulready; *Highland Music*, after Landseer; *The Blind Fiddler*, after

Wilkie; *The Truant*, after Webster; *The Hop Queen*, after Witherington and *Cottage Children*, after Gainsborough. Apart from Messrs F. & R. Pratt, the only firm to show colour-printed pot lids at the 1851 Exhibition was Messrs T. J. & J. Mayer of the Dale Hall Pottery at Longport, Staffordshire. Their stand included 'Various designs for meat pots, printed in colours, under the glaze.' A selection of Pratt multi-coloured printed wares is shown in Plate 19.

Many of the finest Pratt pot lids (and similar multi-coloured printed wares) will be found to bear the signature or initials of Jesse Austin. He was a talented artist and engraver and it is to his skill that the success of this form of ceramic decoration is largely due. Born in February 1806, he was reputedly apprenticed to Davenports, the famous earthenware and porcelain manufacturers of Longport. Later he is said to have set himself up as an engraver to the trade; this is borne out by a reference to him in the *Art Union Magazine* of August 1844:

... we received a few days ago, from Shelton, a plate of ordinary earthenware ... the border contains a Gothic pattern in admirable keeping with the centre, which pictures the ancient gateway of Stow Hall in Suffolk ... The artist by whom the plate is designed and engraved is Mr Jesse Austin of Shelton ...

It should be noted that no mention is made of a manufacturer, only of the designer-engraver, a fact which strongly suggests that Austin was not then tied to Pratts or any other manufacturer. Clarke and other writers have mentioned that at this period he was forced by the bad trade in Staffordshire, to close his independent engraving business and that he was, about 1843 (this year is probably incorrect in view of the above dated quotation), working at a pottery in Leicestershire (possibly that of J. Thompson, at Ashby-de-la-Zouch). About 1848 Jesse Austin was employed by F. & R. Pratt of Fenton to engrave the special copper plates required for the multi-colour prints which were then coming into being. It is recorded that Austin had other engravers working under his direction, but from the original coloured drawings it can be seen that Austin was the master mind behind the art and that he finished and added the telling detail to the copper plates. It must be noted that one Pratt pot lid has the date 31 December 1847 inscribed in gold under the cover, it is, however, difficult to say if this is the date of production.

There is a tradition that Jesse Austin had a serious quarrel with one of the Pratt brothers and that in consequence he left their employment and worked for a year with Messrs Brown-Westhead, Moore & Co. of Cauldon Place, Hanley (working period 1862–1904). The firm produced extremely fine porcelains and earthenware, but I have not been able to trace any pot lids that could be attributed to it with certainty. H. G. Clarke in his 1949 book does list some designs which he attributes to this firm but his reasons are not given.

The Austin–Pratt quarrel was soon patched up, probably as Pratts could not find an engraver to match Austin's skill, and since the market demanded new patterns, old troubles were put aside. Jesse Austin subsequently remained with Pratts until his death in March 1879. The following subjects have been recorded with the master engraver's name or initials; many other subjects are from Austin's designs but do not bear his name on the print (see page 49). Several of the titles do not appear on the print itself but are the names adopted by Mr Clarke for the purposes of his catalogue; the relevant Clarke numbers have been added to this list and relate to the 1960 edition of *The Pictorial Pot Lid Book*. Bracketed numbers on subsequent lists also relate to this work.

Pratt designs bearing Jesse Austin's signature or initials
The Fishbarrow (58).
The Shrimpers (63).
F.M. The Duke of Wellington (162).
The Allied Generals – F.M. Lord Raglan, Gen. Canrobert (168). This design was registered by Pratts in December 1854. (See Plate 19).

22. Mid-Victorian children's plates and mugs, mainly of an educational nature.

Sir Robert Peel (170)
Sebastopol (209).
Meeting of Garibaldi and Victor Emmanuel (211).
War (212 and 219).
Peace (213 and 220).
The Ning Po River (222).
The Seven Ages of Man (230)
Hamlet and his Father's Ghost (231).
The Parish Beadle (236).
Xmas Eve (Registered November 1851) (238). See Plate 19.
The Village Wedding (Registered January 1857) (240).
Our Home (Registered March 1852) (241).
Our Pets (Registered March 1852) (242).
Blind Man's Buff (Registered November 1856) (246).
Snap Dragon (Registered August 1856) (253).
The Skewbald Horse, after Wouverman (277).
I see you, my Boy (311).
The Cottage Children (313).
The Farriers (324).
The First Appeal (329).
Transplanting Rice (332)
Fording the Stream (335).
Girl with Grapes (345).

The Poultry Woman (349).
The Picnic (354).
The Irishman (357).
The Red Bull Inn (359).
A Letter from the Diggings (360).
Valentine's Day (360).
The Listener (363).
The Waterfall (365).

Objects other than Pot Lids
  'The Last In' (412). 1851 Exhibition subject.
  'The Hop Queen' (414). 1851 Exhibition subject.
  'The Bully' (415). Not listed in the 1851 Catalogue but of the same
    series as the others here listed.
  'The Blind Fiddler' (417). 1851 Exhibition subject.
  'Highland Music' (418). 1851 Exhibition subject.
  'Christ in the Cornfield' (424). 1851 Exhibition subject.

It will be observed that I have noted against several of the Austin signed Pratt pot lids that the design was registered; this fact is very important for it enables us to date accurately the year that these patterns were *first* introduced and, in several cases, the name of the manufacturer can be checked. Unfortunately most of the early registered designs were in the name of

23. A selection of
inexpensive
creamware, mostly
Wedgwood
c. 1770–1800.

the retailer who sold the contents of the jar. The following list gives in chronological order the various pot lid type subjects that were registered under the Design Registration Act, with relevant notes.

3 April 1850. Covered 'Sunflower Pomatum' pot, garden scene with figures round base, sunflower top with name of the applicant James King of 13a, Hanway Street London.

23 October 1850. Pot lid, exterior view of the 1851 Exhibition. Registered by Crosse and Blackwell (potted meat manufacturers), Soho Square, London. These 6-oz jars have 'No. 20' impressed in the base.

14 February 1851. Pot lid. Houses of Parliament. Registered by John Cliff Quince of Cheapside, London.

26 February 1851. Pot lid, interior view of the 1851 Exhibition. Registered by J. C. Quince, as above.

17 November 1851. Pot lid, 'Xmas Eve'. Registered by Thomas Jackson of Strangeways, Manchester. (Thomas Jackson's name occurs on several pot lids and may be mistaken for the artist's or engraver's name. In an 1852 Directory he is described as a chemist and druggist; in an 1855 advertisement he is recorded as a 'manufacturer of perfumes and fancy goods'. There are good grounds for believing that some, if not all, designs registered in the name of Thomas Jackson were made by Pratts). This and other subjects bear Jesse Austin's initials, as well as Jackson's name.

29 March 1852. 2 Pot lids, 'Our Pets' and 'Our Home', registered by Thomas Jackson of Manchester. See note above.

1 July 1852. Pot lid, 'The Parish Beadle'. Registered by Thomas Jackson, see note above.

29 December 1854. Pot lid, 'The Allied Generals'. Registered by F. & R. Pratt & Co., the manufacturers. See Plate 19.

12 March 1856. Design for jar etc., hunting scene (not multi-coloured). Registered by F. & R. Pratt & Co., the manufacturers.

12 August 1856. Pot lid, 'Snap Dragon' (family game). Registered by F. & R. Pratt & Co., the manufacturers.

19 August 1856. Design for jar etc., hunting scene (not multi-coloured). Registered by F. & R. Pratt & Co., the manufacturers.

7 November 1856. Pot lid, 'Blind Man's Buff'. Registered by F. & R. Pratt & Co., the manufacturers.

15 January 1857. Pot lid, 'The Village Wedding'. Registered by F. & R. Pratt & Co., the manufacturers.

17 December 1870. Bird subject (swallow) pot lid design. Registered in the name of Bates, Elliot & Co. See Plate 21.

18 August 1871. Potted Meat Pot, shape only. Registered in the name of F. & R. Pratt & Co., the manufacturers.

11 June 1873. 2 designs for Pot lids, 'Injury' and 'Revenge'. Registered in the name of Bates, Elliot & Co., of the Dale Hall Works, Burslem. See Plate 21.

1 January 1874. 3 designs found on Pot lids, 'Summer' and 'Autumn' (children in landscape) and a girl and child in landscape with a goat (number 339 in Mr Clarke's book). Registered in the name of Bates, Elliot & Co., as above. See Plate 21.

The last five registered designs can be linked with Messrs T. J. & J. Mayer of Dale Hall, Longport who showed at the 1851 Exhibition 'Various designs for meat pots, printed in colours, under the glaze.' The Mayer firm was in being from c. 1843 to 1855 (previously Thomas and John Mayer), and from this date there was a succession of partnerships at Dale Hall: Mayer Bros. and Elliot (1856–8); Mayer and Elliot (1858–61); Elliot Bros. (1862); Liddle Elliot & Son (1862–70); Bates Elliot & Co. (1870–5); Bates Walker & Co. (1875–8); Bates, Gildea and Walker (1878–81); Gildea and Walker (1881–5) and James Gildea (1885–8). Up to 1888 the latter firm was still advertising: '. . . Perfumists, Druggists and artists ware.' The only marked multi-coloured printed objects by T. J. & J. Mayer known to me are some rare and very fine rectangular plaques, some of which bear a view of Crosse and Blackwell's Soho Square premises with advertising matter below. They bear the impressed mark T. J. & J. MAYER, LONGPORT and illustrate that Mayer enjoyed business with this well-known firm of paste makers, etc.

In 1870, 1873 and 1874 Messrs Bates Elliot & Co. registered at the London Patent Office six designs for pot lids and at the 1871 Exhibition they had shown 'potted meat boxes'. It can be proved that the multi-coloured printing process was used by one of the firms, Liddle Elliot & Son (1862–70), which operated at Dale Hall between T. J. & J. Mayer and Bates Elliot & Co. At least three such colour prints occur on jugs bearing Liddle Elliot & Son's registration mark. One print of sea shells occurs both on these documentary marked jugs of c. 1863 and on pot lids (see Plate 17).

It is very likely that the firms listed above, from Mayer at the time of the 1851 Exhibition to Bates Elliot & Co. in the 1870s, manufactured coloured pot lids of the type we now call Pratt. An enterprising collector could well make his mark by differentiating between the Pratt subjects and those produced by other potters, and in this task he will be helped by Clarke's 1949 *Centenary Pot Lid Book*. It should be borne in mind that all designs bearing Jesse Austin's signature or initials are likely to have been produced by F. & R. Pratt & Co.; these are listed on page 44. Rarely does a Pratt pot lid bear the printed 'Pratt, Fenton' mark. The following subjects were almost certainly issued by one, or more, of the Dale Hall firms:

Autumn (342). See Plate 21.
Bacchanalians at Play (379). Two subjects.
Bear Pit at Regent's Park (6). (The same subject with slight variations was issued by Pratts. The Pratt examples have trees at the left instead of a dome roof.) See Plate 20.
Boar Hunt (262).
Buckingham Palace (176).
Bull Fight (244).
Conway Castle (217).

Drayton Manor (179). See Plate 20.
False Move (251). (Pratts issued the same subject, with the
  addition of a barrel and broom at the right hand edge.)
Fish Market (57). See Plate 20.
Fix or Draughts (256).
Funeral of the late Duke of Wellington (163).
Houses of Parliament (183).
Injury (50). See Plate 21.
Kingfisher (296).
Mending Nets (56). See Plate 20.
New York Fair (142).
Osborne House (182). See Plate 20.
Pegwell Bay (24).
Pheasant Shooting (261).
Revenge (51).
Sea Shells (52). See Plate 17.
Strasburg (331). See Plate 20.
Summer (342). See Plate 21.
Swallow (297). See Plate 21.
Vine Girl (339). See Plate 21.
Windsor Castle (178).
Youth and Age (366).

These and many other subjects will be found on plates, dishes, jars, jugs, vases, etc. Examples with painted pattern numbers – 3729, etc., or with impressed month and year numbers $\frac{3}{66}$ are by Mayer or one of their successors. An example of 'Revenge' bearing under the cover the registration mark used by Bates, Elliott & Co. in 1873 has also impressed into the base 'B.E. & Co.'. This initial mark is very rare.

Messrs C. T. Maling of Newcastle-upon-Tyne (c. 1859–90) made Pratt-type pots as is proved by a base in my own collection which bears their initial mark (within a triangle) moulded in relief. This is the only marked example known to me, but unfortunately it was divorced from its top when purchased and one has no means of telling the pattern of the decorative top with which it was issued. This may have been printed in one colour rather than in several. Jugs with multi-colour prints bear the initial mark of Morgan, Wood & Co. of Burslem c. 1860–70 and Charles Hobson of Burslem c. 1865–75. Printed wares bearing the name WEDGEWOOD with the middle 'E' or the initials W.S. & Co. were made at Stockton-on-Tees.

It will be found that the pot lids that can be proved to be of Pratt manufacture are of better design than the others. The engraving is more natural, the black outline, shading, etc., is not as apparent as in some of the other designs (apart from the best from the Dale Hall firms) and the colouring is of a warm and richer nature.

The collector who needs to keep within the price suggested by the title of this book cannot be expected to collect the full range of pot lid subjects; he would be well advised to limit his collection to one of the main subjects. These have been divided by Mr Clarke into the following subdivisions: Bear motifs (these generally occur on early pot lids); Geographical subjects; Personal Adornment subjects; Floral designs; Exhibition views; Portraits; Historic pictures; Old English scenes; Animal and Bird subjects; Pictorial and Landscape subjects.

Many of the earlier pot lids include the name (and often the address) of the druggist, the selling agent or the manufacturer of the contents of the pot. A very interesting collection could be formed of these named examples and the collector could carry out research on each firm, its working period, etc. My own choice would be to collect examples that show the different contents that these pots were made to contain. Several will be found bearing the name of their contents; a few examples will show the scope of such a collection: 'Bear's Grease Perfumed'; 'Cherry Tooth Paste'; 'Chocolate Paste'; 'Cold Cream of Roses'; 'Crystallized Honey Cream'; 'Naples Shaving Paste'; 'Sunflower Pomatum'; 'Venetian Pomade', etc. Many of the normal unnamed pot lids contained meat and fish pastes of various types. Some interesting early covered pots can be found decorated with ordinary one-colour printed patterns. I have a very attractive 'Fine Tooth Paste' covered pot with the very rare impressed mark 'MAW'. This was purchased at the 1963 Brighton Antiques Fair for two pounds ten shillings. I also have a small pot which is inscribed 'Lip Salve'. Prints at the Victoria and Albert Museum indicate that several of these early designs were engraved by engravers to the trade, not by manufacturers.

All the covered pots discussed are made of earthenware and are therefore opaque. The new collector will find several covered pots of similar shape which are of translucent porcelain; they are are often hand-painted and have a coloured ground. These pots are from bedroom dressing-table sets (trinket sets) and were originally sold in various sizes on a porcelain tray, with matching ring-stands, pin-trays, etc. Most manufacturers of the period, both English and Continental, made such toilet sets. The collector must also be on his guard against buying objects which, at first sight, appear to be decorated by the multi-coloured printed process but, in reality, have a black print which has been coloured over by hand. On close inspection brush marks will be seen on coloured-over specimens, and the workmanship is often poor as such pieces were inexpensive and painted by child labour.

Several pots and pot-lid-type subjects may have been produced by a Staffordshire potter not generally linked with this type of ware – John Lockett. His stand at the 1862 International Exhibition included 'Jars and covers, of a variety of grounds in blue, olive, turquoise, maroon, pink, mat blue, &c., with gold lines, Tamarind jars, richly ornamented and gold labels, cold cream pots and covers, labelled, &c. . . .' These may have been decorated with single colour prints.

The collector of Staffordshire pot lids can hardly proceed without a copy of Harold George Clarke's *The Pictorial Pot Lid Book* (1960). The main catalogue section lists and illustrates over four hundred and fifty varieties and a companion booklet gives a list of prices. It should be noted that these prices are for undamaged examples of superb colouring. The collector should resist the urge to purchase cracked or poor specimens at any price, unless he is concerned only with the printed design which of course is not affected by slight damage to the earthenware.

Indispensable as Mr Clarke's 1960 book is, the author made several errors of fact. I will mention some of these, both to warn the collector and to show that information should always be checked by the inquiring collector; he should not accept everything he is told. On page 18 Mr Clarke, while describing the colour printing process, indicates that the coloured design from each of the different copper plates was applied to the cover *separately*. Modern examples are produced in this manner but it would appear, from the patents of the period, that in the originals, the design was built up on to one sheet of transfer tissue, which was then applied in its complete form to the unglazed cover in one operation. Such statements in patents as '. . . the successive impressions are made by the several plates on one paper, the subject will be then completed for transferring to the ware', confirm this point in theory but it is not known which system was employed in practice.

Mr Clarke states that the Official Catalogue of the 1851 Exhibition discloses that John Ridgway & Co. and William Ridgway were – 'exhibitors of this new process of decorating pottery'. This is not so; the entry for John Ridgway & Co. does not include any reference to an underglaze multi-colour printing process, and the entry for William Ridgway relates to wares decorated by coloured clay introduced while the body was still soft – no printing was involved.

On page 47 of his book, Mr Clarke suggests that pot lids with shell motifs were ordered by Tatnell & Son of Pegwell Bay and that the motifs were shells found at Pegwell Bay. Shell patterns were normal decorative motifs and were a very popular mode of decoration. As the selfsame shell prints occur on ornamental jugs (see Plate 17), door fittings, finger plates, etc., it is difficult to believe that they were all made to the order of a 'purveyor of shrimps' as Messrs Tatnell & Son were styled.

Mr Clarke lists on page 281 a plate decorated with 'Roman Landscape and River Scene . . . from the Wedgewood [*sic*] pottery'. Plates of this kind were made by William Smith & Co. of the Stafford Pottery, Stockton-on-Tees, Yorkshire, before 1855, and they illustrate the fact that the multi-coloured printing process was also practised outside Staffordshire. This firm used the word 'Wedgewood' as a mark. Colour printed plates were also made by Livesley, Powell & Co. of Hanley, Staffordshire in the 1851–66 period.

The popularity of multi-coloured pot lids had waned by the early 1880s and less expensive methods of colour printing had been introduced. However, Pratt's multi-coloured wares were still attracting attention, for we find in 1897 the following account of china displayed for sale on the Victoria Pier, Blackpool:

'a corner display of Messrs F. & R. Pratt's ware printed in colours, which always looks chaste and nice, tobacco jars, small pots, vases, &c., being the principal items.'

As pot lids became the subject of the collector's search (as early as 1897) and acquired a value far above the cost of manufacture, reproductions were made by firms still possessing the original copper plates. Messrs Coalport China Ltd today possess many of Pratt's original Victorian copper plates. In a pre-war wholesaler's catalogue reproduction pot lids were listed in 'assorted designs' in wooden frames at 10s. each (subject to trade discount) and unframed at 5s. each. These reproductions are generally pale, lacking much of the rich colour of the originals. The earthenware body is more compact and harder than that of the old examples, so that a reproduction will give a clearer 'ring' when struck with a coin. Most recent post-war reproductions of pot lids bear printed inscriptions which indicates that they are not originals. A modern reproduction of one of Pratt's originals is before me now and bears inside the lid this printed inscription:

'The Picture on this lid is one of a series printed from original engravings used for ye Old English Pot Lids now so highly valued by Collectors, and first made in Staffordshire 1847–1870.'

Other reproductions were issued by Kirkhams Ltd of Stoke-on-Trent and may be marked in the following manner: 'Reproduced from the original plate for the Jesse Austin process 1845–70 Kirkhams Ltd, Stoke-on-Trent', or 'Coloured Prints from the Original Engravings by Jesse Austin 1757. Reproduced by Kirkhams Ltd Stoke-on-Trent, England.' The inscriptions are printed inside the lid and I have been offered these late examples with the tell-tale inscription painted over, or with the cover mounted in a wooden frame in such a way that the back is covered. Many of these late Kirkham re-issues have two suspension holes in the top edge; these do not appear on the originals. The Kirkham re-issues also have a flat top, not domed as are the old ones. The collector should soon learn to distinguish all reproductions with little trouble. The originals offer wide scope for the collector and while many rarities will certainly cost more than five pounds, a good collection can be formed without exceeding this modest sum. There is always the chance of a lucky purchase of a rare example. I recently purchased an example for two pounds which is 'catalogued' in Mr Clarke's book at twenty pounds.

Selection of English pressed glass of the so-called "slag" type made by Sowerby and other manufacturers. See Chapter 8.

A colored 1887 advertisement for Samuel Clarke's "Fairy Lamps" showing designs—Nos. 87-97.

Victorian glass "Fairy Lamps" including fancy forms and quilted satin effect, bottom row. A night light is shown in one base. See Chapter 9.

Selection of typical Victorian scenic paperweights. See Chapter 10.

Messrs Puttick and Simpson hold important sales of Pot lids from time to time. In December 1963 they sold the important Garner collection and in a series of sales held in 1964 and 1965 the famous Lambert collection was dispersed. In general, the prices given for the rarer covers, especially those in good condition, were higher than the prices given in H. G. Clarke's *The Pot Lid Recorder* (1955 edition).

The Garner and Lambert collections included an interesting series of coloured drawings by Jesse Austin and depicting patterns engraved on pot lids, etc. According to notes on the back of two of these in my own collection, the drawings came from a book discovered at the Pratt factory. I have listed the designs for which drawings are known as it may safely be taken that these designs will occur on Pratt pot lids rather than on examples made by other manufacturers. The bracketed numbers, where given, relate to entries in H. G. Clarke's *The Pictorial Pot Lid Book* (1955 and 1960). Many of the titles are adopted and do not appear on the design.

1 Alas! Poor Bruin
2 Bear attacked by Dogs
4 Bear Hunting
6 Bear Pit
9 Bears at School
13 Shooting Bears
19 Bear, Lion and Cock
30 Belle Vue – Pegwell Bay
53 Herring Fishing: Hauling Trawl
55 Herring Fishing: Landing the Catch
58 The Fishbarrow
63 The Shrimpers
64 Sea Nymph with Trident
91 Uncle Tom and Eva
101 The Mirror
102 The Toilette
105 Lady Reading Book
106 Lady with Hawk
109 Lady, Boy and Mandoline
110 Lady Fastening Shoe
143 Dublin Industrial Exhibition, 1853
147 Philadelphia Exhibition
Interior view of Independence Hall, Philadelphia
153 The Late Prince Consort
157 King Edward and Queen Alexandra on their Marriage in 1863
168 Allied Generals
170 Sir Robert Peel
174 The Blue Boy
181 Sandringham, the Seat of H.R.H. the Prince of Wales
185 St Paul's Cathedral and River Pageant
188 Strathfieldsaye
196 The New Blackfriars Bridge

197 Thames Embankment
200 Alexandra Palace, 1873
201 Trafalgar Square
202 Holborn Viaduct
209 Sebastopol
210 The Battle of the Nile
211 Meeting of Garibaldi and Victor Emmanuel
212 War (shaped oblong)
213 Peace (shaped oblong)
218 The Chin-Chew River
219 War (circular)
220 Peace (circular)
221 Harbour of Hong Kong
222 The Ning Po River
226 Shakespeare's House, Henley Street, Stratford-on-Avon
227 Shakespeare's Birthplace, Stratford-on-Avon
228 Shottery. The Residence of Anne Hathaway, Shakespeare's wife
229 Church of the Holy Trinity, Stratford-upon-Avon
230 The Seven Ages of Man
231 Hamlet and his Father's Ghost
232 The Village Wakes
236 The Parish Beadle
238 Xmas Eve
239 The Swing
240 The Village Wedding
241 Our Home
242 Our Pets
245 The Enthusiast
246 Blind Man's Buff
249 Dangerous, Skating
253 Snap Dragon
254 The Best Card
256 A Fix
259 The Sportsman
260 The Game Bag
263 Children Sailing boat in Tub
265 Good Dog
266 Contrast
269 Deerhound Guarding Cradle
270 The Begging Dog
272 Both Alike
277 The Skewbald Horse
308 Dutch Winter Scene
309 The Faithful Shepherd
310 H.R.H. the Prince of Wales Visiting the Tomb of Washington
311 I see you, my Boy
312 A French Street Scene
313 Cottage Children
316 Lady, Boy and Goat
318 The Old Water Mill
321 Deer Drinking
322 The Rivals

324 The Farriers
327 The Times
329 First Appeal
330 Second Appeal
332 Transplanting Rice
333 Vue de la Ville de Strasbourg prise du Port
335 Fording the Stream
337 The Flute Player
341 The Fisher Boy
343 The Maidservant
345 Girl with the Grapes or Sharing the Gains
348 Peasant Boys
349 The Poultry Woman
350 Halt by the Wayside
351 Preparing for the Ride
353 Persuasion
354 The Picnic
357 The Irishman
358 Little Red Riding Hood
359 The Red Bull Inn
360 A letter from the Diggings
363 The Listener
364 The Strawberry Girl
365 The Waterfall
382 The Cattle Drover (shaped oval design)
386 The Donkey's Foal (oblong design)
391 Milking the Cow (oblong design)
393 A Sea Shore Study (oblong design)
396 The Traveller's Departure (oblong design)
397 Tyrolese Village Scene (oblong design)

Other subjects occur on small objects – pin trays, small vases, teawares, etc., rather than on pot lids. These designs for which the original drawings have been preserved are:

369 The Fisherman's abode
370 The Round Tower
381 The Cavalier and the Serving Woman (shaped oblong panel)
383 Continental scene (shaped oblong panel)
387 Driving Cattle (shaped oblong panel)
388 Cows in Stream near Ruins (shaped oblong panel)

389 The Ferry Boat (shaped oblong panel)
390 A Halt near Ruins (shaped oblong panel)
392 The Muleteer (shaped oblong panel)
394 The Stone Bridge (shaped oblong panel)
395 The Stone Jetty (shaped oblong panel)
398 Village scene on the Continent (shaped oblong panel)
399 The Windmill (shaped oblong panel)
400 The Wooden Bridge (shaped oblong panel)
401 Uncle Tom and Eva (oval panel)
402 Uncle Tom (oval panel)
404 Passing the Pipe (oblong, trefoil ends)
405 The Smokers (oblong, trefoil ends)

Some fine large designs occur on plaques, bread platters, comports, plates and dishes. Jesse Austin's coloured drawings for the following subjects are preserved:

412 The Last in (school)
413 The Truant
414 The Hop Queen
415 The Bully
416 Landscape and River scene (near Llangollen)
417 The Blind Fiddler
418 Highland Music
419 The Travelling Knife Grinder
422 The Rustic Laundrywoman
423 The Mountain Stream
424 Christ in the Cornfield
431 The Spanish Dancers
432 The Two Anglers (Welsh River scene)

Some other Austin drawings are known but the subjects have not been discovered on Pratt pot lids or other wares.

The Pot Lid Circle (or to give it the full name) The Colour Printed Pottery Collectors Association, was founded early in 1965; its objects are to stimulate and encourage research and interchange of views between members. The Secretary is Mr J. Elvy of Vines, Hildenborough, Kent, who will be pleased to give pot lid collectors further information. I am grateful to the President, Mr D. Jenkins for checking the draft of this chapter and for making several helpful corrections.

CHAPTER SEVEN

CERAMIC MISCELLANY

In this chapter various types of low-priced ceramics will be listed in alphabetical order.

CHILDREN'S PLATES, etc.

The potters of the early Victorian era produced a charming range of small size plates, transfer printed, with subjects suitable for children. Some patterns depict scenes from the Bible, others illustrate events in nursery rhymes or songs, others again show sports or pastimes; many illustrate virtues and several others are of an educational nature – alphabet plates, for instance. These are all most decorative and have an unpretentious charm (see Plate 22).

Originally the plates and rarer mugs must have been sold very cheaply at country fairs but today they are rightly being sought out and collected. Most were made at the smaller Staffordshire potteries and few examples bear a factory mark.

An exception to the rule that most children's plates are un-marked occurs on the specimens made by William Smith & Co. of the Stafford Pottery at Stockton-on-Tees. This firm used many impressed or printed marks incorporating the initials 'W. S. & Co.' or with the name in full. The words 'Wedgwood' (or 'Wedgewood') or 'Queens Ware' occur frequently on these Stockton examples. Some good, decorative, earthenware children's plates were made by William Smith & Co. and as we can judge by the German inscriptions on several specimens, the firm exported these wares.

COSTUME

A very varied collection of Victorian ceramics could be formed of wares showing costume of the period. They include printed patterns of all types and in all price ranges, hand-painted wares or figures and groups. Surprisingly little attention was paid to depicting costume of the period on hand-painted wares, where the vogue was for Watteau type figures or other 18th-century styles. Nevertheless when Victorian costume is shown the result is quite charming and, as fashions change rapidly, a practised collector could date the ware by the costume and hair style to narrow limits. Parian figures offer a considerable number of costume styles ranging through the Victorian era.

In a collection of this type the price of the pieces will vary considerably, from printed earthenwares of an inexpensive nature to fine quality porcelains, painted by the foremost artists of the day, at the other end of the financial scale. Some charming figures and groups of children in Kate Greenaway style costume were modelled by James Hadley for the Royal Worcester Porcelain Company in the 1880s. (See *Victorian Porcelain*, 1961.)

CREAM-WARE

Creamware was the staple English earthenware body from about 1770 to about 1820. Perfected by Josiah Wedgwood, it replaced the earlier salt glazed stonewares and, when exported in large quantities to the Continent, forced many of the faience factories there to close, or to imitate it. Josiah Wedgwood called his refined creamware 'Queens Ware', to denote the fact that he had Royal patronage, but nearly every potter of the late 18th century produced good quality creamware (see Plate 23).

Choice specimens today rightly command a high price but a very interesting collection could be formed of objects purchased for five pounds or less. The scope is so large and the amount produced so huge that even at this price the collector would probably find more specimens than he could house. He would have to specialize and collect marked examples; the possibilities here probably exceed a hundred different marks. There are specimens without decoration, those that depend on their good design and potting, or examples that bear simple enamelled border motifs. These border patterns of floral design or of formal scroll work, etc., are most attractive and are grossly undervalued today. Good marked Wedgwood plates of this type and of the 1780–1800 period can be purchased with little trouble and for a few pounds.

It may well surprise readers that antique creamwares should be included in this book on low-priced wares. That it is possible to purchase good quality creamwares at under five pounds can be easily proved; this is no doubt due to the long period during which it was the standard body and to the number of potters that were producing it day after day. Furthermore, it was not intended only for the rich; most people could afford the plainer types of creamware. In 1812, a London retailer could supply a 'family crate' of Queens Ware for £3 13s. 6d. including the packing. This crate included one hundred and eighty-three units made up as follows:

21 dishes in assorted sizes.
60 large plates.
18 soup plates.
18 pie plates.
18 cheese plates.
 1 soup tureen, stand and ladle.
 4 sauce tureens, stands and ladles.
 4 covered dishes.
 2 salad bowls.
 6 baking dishes.
 1 fish drainer.
 2 mustards.
 2 peppers.
 3 salts.
 4 chamber vases.
 2 water ewers.
 8 kitchen ewers.
 6 jugs.
 2 mugs.

It must be admitted that the price of £3 13s. 6d. quoted above was for undecorated creamware but the corresponding prices for decorated wares were not greatly in excess of this sum:

Blue edge Queens Ware service £5 15s. 6d.
Green edge Queens Ware service £6 16s. 6d.
Brown line or 'Wedged' ware £6 6s. od.
Best blue and white English Nankeen £7 17s. 6d.

The standard reference book on creamwares is Donald Towner's *English Cream-coloured Earthenware*, 1957. This will be found to give illustrations and details of most types of creamware and its more important manufacturers.

CUPS

An interesting and instructive collection can be formed of 18th-century porcelain cups. These represent the only 18th-century items that can be consistently found at under five pounds.

Representative specimens of all English porcelain factories, of the various periods and styles of decoration can be discovered. In early Bow porcelain, for example, one can find white specimens with moulded prunus sprays, examples decorated in underglaze blue only and cups decorated with overglaze enamel decoration.

There is probably no better way to know thoroughly the various English (or Continental) porcelain factories and their characteristics than to gather together a representative collection of cups. Once you can tell the difference between a Bow blue and white cup and a Lowestoft one, or between a Bristol hard paste cup and a Plymouth one, then your ground work is sound and can be enlarged upon. All would-be collectors of 18th-century English ceramics should form a collection of typical cups: many costly mistakes could be avoided if they did so. A selection of Worcester cups is shown in Plate 24.

There is the added advantage that matching odd saucers can sometimes be found especially if the collection of cups is large. A cup costing 30s. can be 'married' to a £3 saucer (the price of odd saucers is normally much higher than that of a cup) and the resulting cup and saucer sold for about ten pounds. With luck, the sale of a few matching cups and saucers can repay the expenditure on a whole collection of cups. I do not, however, suggest that this should be the reason for collecting cups; the main reasons are enjoyment and the educational value of the pursuit.

The collector of cups, seeking a ground work to 18th-century English porcelains, and within reach of London, will be well advised to make frequent visits to the Victoria and Albert Museum and inspect the vast collections displayed on the top floor. He should also take advantage of the porcelain sales held at Messrs Sotheby's and Messrs Christie's London sale-rooms. The lots are accurately described in the catalogue and, most

24. Worcester porcelain cups
c. 1755–1800, mostly with
crescent or square mark in
underglaze blue.

important, the collector is able to handle the objects. The cup collector will require one or two standard reference books which point out the characteristics of each factory or period; these will include *English Pottery and Porcelain* by W. B. Honey (5th edition, 1962); *18th Century English Porcelain* by George Savage (1952); *English Blue and White Porcelain of the 18th century* by Bernard Watney (1963); *English Porcelain 1745–1850* (1965).

'EARLY TO BEDS'

This name is often applied to an amusing range of small porcelain groups, with titles such as 'Twelve months after marriage' and 'Last in Bed to put out the light' and many other subjects mainly concerned with married life or courtship (see Plates 26 and 27). They are of German porcelain but are featured in this work because I am informed that many are sold as being of Staffordshire manufacture and in some cases the inscription 'Made in Germany' has been removed to keep up the pretence. Later examples are Japanese and sometimes bear the inscription 'Made in Japan'.

These groups have become very fashionable and are often given to newly weds as an amusing 'gimmick'. At the present time a number of collectors are endeavouring to gather together a complete series. Several hundred different designs were produced and many are extremely rare, although originally they were shipped to England in large quantities and sold very cheaply in Bazaars, etc.

Not all specimens originate from one firm but the vast majority of models were issued by one manufacturer. These specimens often bear a shield device containing an upraised hand; this mark is usually impressed but I have examples on which it is moulded in relief or printed over the glaze.

25. Porcelain ornaments bearing the shield mark of Conta & Boehme. Large figure 9″ high.

One 'specialist' in these groups was very happy to inform me that these examples with shield-shaped marks were made in Elbogen in Germany. Having learned many years ago to check all information for myself, I sought to confirm this point. Several mark books list a shield with arm as that of Springer & Co. of Elbogen, but the mark given was that of a shield of simple outline with convex sides rather than the ornate one with concave sides that occurred on these groups; moreover the elbow of the arm on the Elbogen mark pointed downwards, on the figures it pointed upwards. I was back where I started except that I now knew that the Elbogen attribution was probably an error, originated by someone who had not compared the marks closely.

Luckily, the relevant firm was of some duration for I found the exact mark recorded in a German trade journal of 1907. The entry, with mark, is reproduced below and proves that the mark on the 'Early to bed group' was that used by Messrs Conta and Boehme of Possneck, Saxony. The specialities of this firm include bazaar goods in all price ranges – groups, figures, tobacco jars, cigar holders, match strikers, menu holders, etc. – exported to all countries. The firm claimed to have been established in 1790; the extent of their export trade can be gauged by the fact that they exhibited at the 1880 Melbourne Exhibition.

I have been unable to trace any definite contemporary

26. German porcelain groups of 'Early to Bed' type made by Conta & Boehme of Possneck and bearing the firm's shield shaped mark.

references to this type of porcelain group, though a trade review of Messrs Frank Tuhten & Co.'s imported wares in 1899 may be relevant as the price and kind of selling outlet could well be appropriate:

Messrs Tuhten & Co have a large assortment of new figure ware expressly intended for what are known as 'sixpenny lines' in the English market. These are especially suitable for fancy stalls, bazaars, watering places and holiday resorts.

This firm advertised '1d., 6d. and 1s. china figures. . . . Novelties arrive continually.' Firms other than Conta and Boehme made similar groups and figures, some are marked with the initials E.B.S.

The Conta and Boehme groups were made over a long period. The earliest are heavier than the later examples, the bases have a shallow recess and the model number was roughly incised. The shield mark was rarely used at this period. Later examples bear the shield mark impressed, and the model number was also impressed rather than incised. From about 1891 the words 'Made in Germany' may be added; the mark is often printed at this period rather than impressed or moulded in relief. The later groups are of noticeably lighter weight and the bases are hollow because of changing methods of manufacture. Several of these little figures were intended as match holders and the rough striking surface can often be seen at the back or sides.

An amusing collection of pieces could be formed at little cost although as the collection proceeds and rare models are sought, the price will be higher. Prices for even the commonest models

Conta & Boehme,
Porzellanfabrik u. Dampf-Gipsfabrik in P ö s s n e c k (⟁ ⴕ ☙), Sachsen-Meinigen. — T.-A.: Conta. — ☙ Nr. 3. — Inh.: Kommerzienrat Max Conta, Hermann u. Robert Conta. — Bankkonten: Reichsbank u. Deutsche Bank.

Fabrikat in Hartporzellan: Luxus- u. Phantasieartikel für In- u. Ausland. — Spez. u. Export: Basarartikel in allen Preislagen, Kandelaber, Tafelaufsätze, Jardinieren, Uhrenständer, Spiegel, Gruppen, Pagoden u. sonstige Wackelfiguren, Spitzenfiguren, Figuren, Heiligenfiguren, Weihkessel, Tiere, Tabaksdosen, Zigarrenständer u. -Schalen, Aschenständer, Streichfeuerzeuge, Menuhalter, Senfmenagen, Schreibzeuge. Schmuck- u. Spiegeldosen, Vasen, Großartikel, Badekinder, Puppenköpfe, Zeugpuppen, Wandreliefs, Leuchter, Jardinieren zum Hängen. Ferner Fabrikation von feinstem Alabaster-, Modell-, Form-, Stuck-, Bau- u. Düngegips.

Entry from German trade journal showing the shield mark found on many small porcelain groups. Conta & Boehme's specialities, bazaar goods in all price ranges are also listed.

have doubled in recent years. Bristowe's book 'Victorian China Fairings' offers a good pictorial guide to these groups but the text regarding attribution of the manufacturers and the mark is inaccurate.

GLAZE EFFECTS

The collector with an interest in chemical effects, or one seeking decorative objects could, with advantage, gather together a selection of wares with lustres and special glaze effects. Late in the 19th century several potters were experimenting with these. Most examples are unique, for the firing temperature and atmosphere affected each batch to a remarkable degree, even when the glaze was chemically the same, which it seldom was.

The early wares of Bernard Moore are neglected by most collectors; they are signed with the initials 'B.M.' or with the name in full. Examples are shown in Plate 29. The wares of William De Morgan are largely out of the price range covered in this book, but they should be purchased where possible. Hugh Wakefield includes a chapter on this potter in his *Victorian Pottery* (1962). The Pilkington 'Royal Lancastrian' lustre and glaze effect wares produced from 1897 to 1938 are likewise extremely decorative and a good investment. Details of the marks and artist's signs are given in my *Encyclopaedia of British Pottery and Porcelain Marks* (1964).

Many studio potters also produce attractive glaze effects, as do some commercial potteries such as Josiah Wedgwood & Sons Ltd; their experimental glaze effects by Norman Wilson have been avidly collected in this country and in America.

GREEN GLAZED EARTHENWARES

Some charming green glazed earthenwares may be purchased at little cost, certainly below that which their decorative merit would suggest. Wedgwood and other 18th-century potters made dessert sets and other wares in this style. The plates, dishes, etc., have a raised moulded design, often of leaf motifs and the applied semi-translucent green glaze serves to accentuate the design in a subtle manner (see Plate 30). Factory marks can be found on many of these wares which were produced during most of the 19th century and have been continued up to the present day by Messrs Josiah Wedgwood & Sons Ltd. Some fine green glazed wares of the 1806–40 period bear the impressed BRAMELD mark and these were made at the Rockingham Works, near Swinton, Yorkshire. Others with the impressed mark COPELAND were made after 1847. The early Wedgwood examples are thinly potted and of very neat workmanship. From 1860 onwards a series of three impressed letters occur on Wedgwood green glazed wares; they are potting marks and give the month and year in which the pieces were made. The key to these year cyphers is given in my *Encyclopaedia of British Pottery and Porcelain Marks* (1964) and in most modern books on Wedgwood

27. Late 19th century, early 20th century slip cast groups of
light weight, hollow bases and printed titles.

wares. From 1907 a number replaces the first letter. A more simple system was started in 1930 and continues to the present day: in this the month is numbered in sequence and the last two numbers of the year are added after the potter's personal mark or letter, so that '1A33' indicates that workman A potted the specimen in January 1933.

Single plates and dishes of green glazed earthenware can be found at very little cost and an interesting and decorative collection formed for less than would be required to purchase one specimen of a more fashionable ceramic style of decoration.

Two similar modes of decoration were introduced in the 19th century. The style known as *Email Ombrant* was popularized at Baron A. du Tremblay's earthenware factory at Rubelles, France and taken up in this country by Wedgwoods in the 1860s. The design was impressed, or made from a mould formed so that portions of the design intended to be dark were recessed. The object, with its intaglio pattern, was then flooded with a semi-translucent glaze (usually green) so that the design was formed in monochrome according to the depth of the coloured glaze in any one place. I have a fine Wedgwood circular plaque with the year mark of 1876 treated in this manner. The pattern is a complicated landscape subject with figures. In general the *Email Ombrant* designs had landscape and figure subjects rather than the leaf and floral motifs of the earlier green glazed wares. It will be appreciated that this form of decoration was suitable only for flat objects such as tiles, panels, plates or dishes, on which the glaze could be applied in a flat, even layer.

Portrait and figure subject tiles were made in this technique in the 1890s by George Cartlidge who then worked for Messrs

Sherwin and Cotton, tile manufacturers of Hanley. Examples may be found with George Cartlidge's signature or initials on the front and Sherwin and Cotton's name on the reverse. George Cartlidge was born in 1868. Several years ago, after buying one of these realistic flat portrait plaques (see Plate 28), I located the artist-modeller living in Derbyshire. The following extracts from two letters tell in his own words, the basic methods of production and details of his ceramic career:

The original is modelled in clay, from this it is cast in plaster, and from that a metal die is high cast. Then from this the tile is made in a tile press.

After the initial firing it is dipped in a special tinted glaze, and then placed with a spirit level (the tile must be perfectly flat or the glaze would flow to one side and ruin the effect) in the kiln for its final firing. The result is a most realistic picture, resembling a photograph.

Of his career, George Cartlidge wrote:

I started attending the Hanley N. Staffs Art School in 1878. In 1882 I was apprenticed to a firm of Tile Manufacturers to learn the mystery of Art in Tile Decoration. I quickly made progress there and continued at the Art School each evening until 1897. During this period I obtained my Art Master's Certificate and several awards, etc., from South Kensington. After long study I did many Ceramic modelled miniatures and then portrait Tiles. The first important Ceramic Portrait was of W.E.Gladstone in 1898. This was followed by one of Pope Pius 10th and one of Queen Victoria – then I did one of Abraham Lincoln in 1910 – the centenary of his birth.

Following I did a series for Australia including two Maori Chiefs and two Guides women. One of the latter, 'Bella' had a copy presented to her by the Australian representative when she was giving a show in Sydney Harbour. During the 1914/18 war I did Ceramic Portraits of Marshall Foch, General Haig, Lord Jellicoe, Admiral Lord Beatty, President Woodrow Wilson, General Smuts, Lloyd George.

In 1919 I was invited to go to America to model a ceramic portrait of the Candidate General Leonard Wood whom I interviewed in Chicago, then I modelled General Harding. I worked for a firm of Tile Manufacturers in Newport, Kentucky doing designs. In my spare time I was painting portraits and other pictures besides doing the Ceramic work.

Have modelled Ceramic portraits of many local people in North Staffs. The last Ceramic Portrait I modelled was of Thomas Hardy, the Novelist in 1924. This I did for myself and the number of copies was limited to 30. I might add that the Ceramic Portraits I modelled in America had to be brought to England to be manufactured.

A typical specimen, a portrait of Queen Victoria, is shown in Plate 28.

LUSTRE WARES

There are three main groups of lustre decorated earthenwares –

28. Portrait plaque modelled by George Cartlidge c. 1897.

copper (gold), silver and pink lustre; this kind of decoration seems to have been confined almost entirely to English potters. The early lustre wares of the 1810–30 period are mostly outside the price range covered in this book. This is especially true of the resist lustre wares in which ornate patterns are produced by a stencil-like process, or by covering the parts to be left unlustred with a material which will resist the lustre.

The names copper, gold, silver and pink lustre are to some extent misleading. Chemically all ceramic lustre is derived from two metals, gold and platinum in solution. The gold lustre, in particular, is to a very high degree translucent, and the colour of the body or ground, over which it is applied, determines the colour: on a dark chocolate ground it appears as a deep rich gold colour termed 'copper' by most collectors. When it is applied over a white or pale ground the same solution gives a very popular and attractive pink lustre, the colour of which can be graduated by applying two or more coatings (some attractive landscape designs were built up in this way). Many gold or copper lustre jugs, etc., appear at first sight to have a white body because a white slip has been applied to the inside of the jug, for the sake of appearance. Bands of white or coloured slip are sometimes applied to the outside of the jug and further decorated: they can be felt as slight protuberances from the copper lustre ground.

The silver lustre was derived from platinum – several writers have stated that it should therefore be called platinum lustre,

29. Selection of early 20th century
Bernard Moore glaze effect vases etc.
Presented to the British Museum in 1902.
Tallest vase 7.9″ high.

but as the potters of the period used the term 'silver' and many examples were made in imitation of silver, I favour the old name. This may be applied over a dark pottery body or on creamware and porcelain. Most of the cheaper all-over silver lustre wares were produced from a dark pottery body, but the finer jugs, etc., have a white or slightly tinted creamware body; the expensive resist and stencilled lustre wares have a white body, and some useful wares have a silver lustre rim. The Sunderland type splash lustre finish is also applied over a white body.

The best-known examples of silver lustre are those completely covered with silver lustre, in imitation of silver ware. The shapes of teapots, etc., are often copied from silver prototypes and these all-over silver lustre earthenwares were no doubt intended to be the poor man's silver. Early wares can seldom be purchased for under seven or eight pounds but as with the copper lustre objects, the later Victorian examples are neglected and cheaper in price.

At the 1851 Exhibition Edwin Deakin of Longton showed silver lustre articles – mouth ewer and basin, coffee pots and teapots, sugar boxes and creamers and Messrs Glover and Colclough of Longton exhibited silver lustre jugs, etc. The directories of the 1830–60 period give many names for lustre

manufacturers but their individual wares cannot be identified. The collector should concentrate on the decorative merits of the ware, rather than academic points.

A very decorative collection of gold or copper lustre wares of the post-1830 period could be formed at small cost and they have a warm, mellow tone that is especially suited to cottage furnishing schemes. The wares are seldom marked and were made by a host of Staffordshire manufacturers (some examples were decorated by specialist lustrers working on blanks made by others); few specimens can be identified with certainty. Messrs Bailey and Batkin of Lane End, Staffordshire specialized in lustred wares from 1814 to 1827: those shipped by this firm to America in 1816 included gold lustre coffee pots, teapots, sugars and creamers.

At a later period John Lockett of Longton made gold lustre wares. His stand at the 1862 Exhibition included 'Gold lustre ware, in every variety, in teacups and saucers, jugs, mugs, ewers and basins, bowls and covers, bowls, vases, teapots, sugar boxes and cream jugs, garden pots and stands, toy cups and saucers, mugs, jugs, etc.'

Several moulded jugs also occur with a coating of copper or gold lustre. One very popular pattern showing a couple dancing the Polka (see Plate 32) is interesting as the early examples bear a diamond-shaped device showing that the design was registered on the 21 April 1852 in the name of George Ray of Longton, Staffordshire.

The collector should be warned that lustre wares bearing the

30. Green glazed earthenwares, left
    to right, Copeland leaf dish *c.* 1860,
    Brameld tureen *c.* 1820, Wedgwood plate
    c. 1865.

name 'Allertons' are of 20th-century date and that reproductions of old lustre jugs are today being made and in some cases sold as antique; Sunderland type splash lustre is also reproduced. The standard work is *Old English Lustre Potters* by W. D. John and Dr Warren Baker, but this is an expensive and rare reference book.

MAJOLICA WARES

Majolica glazed earthenware is, after Parian, the most often encountered kind of Victorian ceramic. Many examples emulate the true Italian Maiolica ware and consist of an opaque coating of tinted glaze over an earthenware body. The term is also widely used to denote the semi-translucent colour-glazed earthenwares, so popular during the middle of the 19th century. The true Italian wares are spelled 'Maiolica'; for the Victorian earthenwares, the spelling is 'Majolica'.

Majolica ware was introduced by Mintons *c*. 1850, in time for the inclusion of many specimens in the 1851 Exhibition. Some fine examples of old Maiolica were copied at Mintons, the chief painters in this style being Thomas Allen and Thomas Kirkby. Special enamels were prepared by Leon Arnoux (Mintons' Art Director) to meet the special glaze and tone requirements of these pieces. The Majolica wares were used for a wide assortment of objects ranging from colossal fountains and staircases to small figures and pin trays. The early Minton objects, especially signed pieces, painted with figure subjects by Allen or Kirkby are today expensive and keenly sought, but many of the small decorative objects are still reasonably priced and well worth the attention of the discriminating collector.

Although Minton's name will always be associated with the Majolica wares, other manufacturers, including Wedgwood, quickly took advantage of its popularity. One of the leading manufacturers of Majolica was Messrs George Jones of the Trent Pottery (and later the Crescent Pottery). George Jones was originally employed at Mintons but established his own factory at Stoke in 1861. He soon won praise for the high quality and diversity of his products, and the firm exhibited at the International Exhibitions, including those at Paris in 1867

31. Two mid-Victorian 'copper lustre' jugs and a 'silver lustre' jug of Meigh type (centre).

and Vienna in 1873. George Jones' Majolica wares were mainly confined to table pieces of unusual form including dessert sets with comports, centrepieces, salad dishes, strawberry dishes and tureens in various original shapes. His examples often bear the impressed monogram of his initials J.G. After 1873 '& Son' occurs in a crescent below the initials.

Another of the lesser-known manufacturers of this ware (and of high class porcelain) was Messrs Brown-Westhead, Moore & Co. (of the Cauldon Place Works, Hanley) of whose exhibits in the Paris Exhibition of 1878 George Augustus Sala wrote:

Another firm of British potters whose manufacture shows a very decided advance and calls for praise, both for artistic beauty of design and excellence of workmanship – they are producers at first hand of some remarkably well executed vases and plaques, displaying rare beauty of form and brilliance of colour, and of a variety of quaintly designed flower-holders, in which birds and animals are felicitously introduced.

These wares generally bear the impressed initials 'B.W.M. & Co.' or the name in full.

Messrs W. Brownfield & Son of Cobridge produced similar high-grade Majolica wares of novel design, with the name in full or with the initials 'W.B.' within a knot. Many lesser manufacturers tended to swamp the market with cheap grade wares. As with so many classes of Victorian ware, the best is very good and the worst extremely bad.

Like those with the white parian body, the coloured glazed Majolica earthenwares are typically Victorian in feeling, and again like parian, the wares are both inexpensive and often very decorative. Such objects as strawberry dishes are especially fine, and suitable for even the most modern of table settings; the monumental size of some specimens is, however, a drawback. Many objects will be found with the diamond-shaped design registration mark (see Chapter 2) which will show the date that the design was first issued.

32. Copper lustre 'Polka' jug. Design registered by George Ray of Longton in April 1852.

MENU HOLDERS

The Victorian table must have been very decorative if the many novelties that were introduced by the manufacturers were used – the menu and place cards, for instance, that were produced by china firms from the 1860s onwards. These can be found in two basic forms – those in which a portion of the object is flat in order that the menu or person's name can be written upon it in pencil, and those in which a normal menu card, or name card, can be placed on a decorative base.

A novel collection of these Victorian menu and place card stands could be formed at low cost. They could be displayed in a small case or wall fitting and used on the table on special occasions. Many of the designs bear the manufacturer's name, or the diamond shaped pattern registration mark (see Chapter 2).

'MOCHA' DECORATED EARTHENWARE

The English 'Mocha' earthenwares constitute one of several interesting and decorative kinds of pottery that are border-line cases for inclusion in a book dealing with objects obtainable at under five pounds. The simpler wares – mugs, jugs, etc., can be purchased in this price range but the rarer pieces now command a higher price.

The characteristic tree-like pattern (see Plate 33) known as Mocha, is produced by the chemical reaction of an acid colourant on an alkaline ground colour. A light coloured alkaline slip is applied to the vessel, normally in the form of a band. To this is applied (before it is dry) a drop of acid colourant termed 'tea', and by chemical reaction it grows quickly into a tree-like design which can be controlled by inclining the object. The normal tree growth is obtained by placing the drop of acid colourant at the bottom edge of the alkaline band and reversing the object so that the drop runs downward rather than across. It will be observed that the tree-like growth stops abruptly at the edge of the alkaline band.

Charles Dickens described the process, when writing of a visit to the Copeland Works at Stoke-on-Trent in 1852:

Jugs and mugs were once more (after shaping, etc.) set upon a lathe and put in motion . . . a man blew the brown colour (the alkaline slip) on them from a blow-pipe as they twirled . . . his daughter with a common brush, dropped blotches of blue upon them in the right places; tilting the blotches upside down, she made them run into rude images of trees . . .

Dickens noted that this type of ware was then 'exported to Africa and used in cottages at home'. The wares were inexpensive as no skilled labour was involved and the objects could be produced with a minimum of trouble. The decoration was all applied before firing and glazing, so that only one firing was required in their manufacture. This fact not only reduced costs, it reduced wastage in firing losses. Mugs were priced at 3s. 6d. a dozen in the 1880s and 1890s against 5s. a dozen for printed examples.

Production of Mocha ware ranged over a century. An example in the Ipswich Museum is illustrated in my *British Pottery and Porcelain* 1780–1850 (1963) and dated 1799, but the ware is described in invoices before this date. In the 1890s illustrated advertisements for it were issued by Messrs C. T. Maling & Sons (of Newcastle-upon-Tyne) and on the evidence of examples seen today the production of Mocha ware must have continued well into the present century.

Many Mocha mugs were made for public house use and were stamped to show that they held the correct measure. Official stamps may be impressed on lead tags fixed to the handles or engraved on the top edges of the articles. The reign initials on these stamps give an approximate guide to the date – V.R. = 1837–1901, E.R. = 1901–10. G.R. = 1910+

J. Arnold Fleming, a practical potter with first-hand knowledge of the manufacture of Mocha ware, wrote in his *Scottish Pottery* (1923) 'Mocha ware has a style all its own, and is probably the most mysterious and extraordinary of all the old fashioned schemes for decorating the pottery used by the country people of a generation or more ago.' Mugs and jugs are the most frequently found objects but many other items also bear this interesting, naïve style of decoration; teasets are known but are very rare. Factory marked wares are extremely rare.

MOULDED JUGS

An interesting range of moulded relief pattern jugs was produced in the 19th century. At first these were in stoneware or

33. 'Mocha' decorated earthenwares *c.* 1840–60.
Godden of Worthing Ltd.

coloured earthenware, and from about 1842 they also occur in white or tinted parian. Today they can be found in nearly every antique or second-hand shop and are usually priced at less than five pounds.

The early specimens often bear self-explanatory copyright marks which include the name of the manufacturer and the date that the design was first published. Manufacturers of this type of jug included Jones and Walley; Charles Meigh; Ridgway & Abington and W. Ridgway & Co. Typical specimens are illustrated in my *British Pottery and Porcelain 1780–1850*. The later parian examples often bear the diamond-shaped pattern registration marks, impressed or printed (see Plate 8).

Such marks were employed from 1842 to 1883, and the key to the month and year of registration is given in Chapter 2. An interesting study of the changes in style of these jugs (and allied objects) can be obtained by the display of these marked examples in chronological order.

The number of different Victorian jug designs is so large that the collection can be divided into classes – figure subjects, floral designs, etc., or a collection can be limited to jugs in one of several ceramic bodies – parian (see Plate 8) stoneware or decorated earthenware.

A good range of moulded jugs is illustrated in Hugh Wakefield's *Victorian Pottery*, 1962.

PARIAN

Of the many ceramic 'bodies', the typically Victorian 'parian' body (or Statuary Porcelain, as it was originally called) must be known to all. As the name suggests, parian, with its unglazed white body, has the appearance of marble, but unlike marble, it is capable of being moulded in its liquid state. It was this characteristic that made it so welcome to the Victorian ceramic manufacturers who could produce large quantities of inexpensive moulded figures and groups. Copies of world-famous sculpture by ancient as well as eminent sculptors of the day were introduced into the humblest of homes as a result of the introduction of the parian body.

Messrs Copeland and Garrett of Stoke-on-Trent introduced this body in the 1840s although other manufacturers were experimenting with similar bodies in the same period. The Art Union magazine dated January 1846 contains an interesting account of early parian wares shown at the Manchester Exposition.

... Of statuettes there are many examples of a character wholly distinct from the class generally known as bisque or pottery figures. The aim has been to imitate, both in material and execution, the artistic excellence and effect of sculpture; and the result has been most successful ... It is impossible to devise more apt or desirable ornaments for the drawing-room.

The Art Union movement, a form of lottery in which works of art were awarded as prizes, did much to popularize parian figures. Judging from the number of examples available today bearing Art Union inscriptions, a vast number of sculptured works, in miniature, must have found their way into the hands of otherwise uninterested parties.

The major manufacturers naturally marked their wares, but owing to the popularity of this inexpensive body, many smaller manufacturers flooded the market with unmarked productions lacking the quality and finish of the marked ones. Apart from their decorative merits these parian figures, busts and groups afford an inexpensive opportunity to collect a form of art typically Victorian in conception.

So popular was the parian body and so readily could it be manufactured by the potters that it was used for wares other than figures and groups. Moulded jugs, vases and centrepieces were made in profusion, as were charming floral encrusted brooches, etc. It could easily be tinted and many jugs were made in two or more colours giving an effect similar to that of Wedgwood's jasper wares. For simplicity of effect, few decorative schemes can equal white parian figures with slight gilt enrichments. Minton's glazed parian ornaments in celadon and white are also very striking.

PHOTO-CERAMICS

With the introduction and development of photography in the last century, several firms and individuals experimented to find processes by which photographic images could be transferred to earthenware, successfully fixed and fired. Messrs Wedgwoods produced good examples of photo-ceramics, as did Mintons and Doultons and some Continental firms. Minton blanks were used by several photographic firms which specialized in this type of work; I have marked Minton plates bearing year cyphers of 1884, still with the original paper labels of the Ceramic, Stained Glass and Vitrified Photograph Company of 19, Finsbury Circus, London, E.C.

This is an interesting subject and collectors will have opportunities to pick up real bargains; examples are by no means common, but when found, specimens are not likely to be highly priced. Dr Helmut Gernsheim in his book *The History of Photography* (1955) touches on this subject and mentions that an unworked patent for firing photographs was taken out as early as 1849 in the names of Fox Talbot and Thomas Malone.

STONEWARE BOTTLES

Decorative and often amusing stoneware bottles made at several potteries during the first half of the 19th-century can often be purchased for a few pounds and are an interesting subject for the new collector.

Several moulded stoneware bottles commemorate special occasions like the Reform Bill and the accession of Queen Victoria. Others are in the form of various objects such as pistols, fish, portraits and figures. The best examples often bear the maker's name – Doulton and Watts (c. 1815–58), Stephen Green of Lambeth (c. 1820–58), Joseph Kishere of Mortlake (c. 1800–43), W. Northern (c. 1847–92), James Stiff of Lambeth (c. 1840–63) and James Stiff & Sons (c. 1863–1913). All these potters had works in London. Similar stoneware bottles were made in other centres, chiefly in the Nottingham district and in Derbyshire.

Typical moulded stoneware bottles are illustrated in J. F. Blacker's *The A.B.C. of English Salt-Glaze Stone-ware* (1922). Hundreds of different designs were made and these can be found today in the most unlikely places.

STUDIO POTTERS

The term 'Studio Potter' covers a large and increasing number of 20th-century potters who produce largely individual hand-made wares, normally earthenware and stoneware rather than porcelain, in studio-like conditions. All operations are carried out by the potter concerned, or by his small team, so that the potter has personal control from start to finish. This is in strong contrast to conditions in a modern factory where the design is conceived by one or more people, passed to others to translate into pottery, and then to the decorators, while it is finally entrusted to others again for the firing processes. The studio potter is normally responsible for all this, and his wares consequently display his personal taste and ability.

Studio potters can today be found in all localities and the collector would be well advised to seek out and patronize these modern craftsmen; their products are the antiques of the future. Apart from their good taste and workmanship, these wares are often unique specimens of one man's craft. I have a reference collection of over one hundred specimens from different modern studio potters. These purchases have given me the greatest pleasure and much useful knowledge.

The work of many famous English studio potters has been avidly collected for many years and their work displayed in art galleries and museums throughout the world. The name of Bernard Leach of St Ives is spoken of in awe wherever pottery is appreciated for its beauty or utility. The new collector will be disappointed if he tries to purchase the work of the 'discovered masters' for their work is usually vouched for before it is displayed or often before it is potted. If available such specimens will be relatively costly. The collector should start his modest collection by visiting a local potter, talking to him and purchasing an example that appeals to his personal taste or requirements. A craftsman is always willing to give advice and help if he knows that one has a genuine interest in his work. I am not suggesting that one should worry a potter while he is throwing a vase or decorating a pot; it is far more civilized to ask questions over a pint of beer in the local pub.

The Craftsmen Potters shop in Lowndes Court, London, W.1, does a real service in showing hundreds of specimens of modern hand-made pottery in one centrally situated shop; the selection is vast, the staff most helpful and the prices extremely modest. The shop is run by the Craftsmen Potters Association, and its members are all practising potters. Many special exhibitions are held in which an individual potter's work is featured, the potter himself being present to demonstrate or talk to the customers. In this way one can meet potters from districts several hundred miles away from one's own happy hunting ground. It would be difficult for any collector with love for clay or craftsmanship to leave the Craftsmen Potters Shop without making at least one purchase. The collector of modern studio pottery is also well served by the Crafts Centre in Hay Hill, 'Primavera' in Sloane Street and 'Anshel' at 33, King's Road, Chelsea. My own collection has been formed largely from purchases made at these four shops or from purchases made direct from the potters' studios.

The collector of modern pottery is strongly recommended to purchase Bernard Leach's *A Potters Book*; he will also find useful information on the 'discovered masters' in three recent reference books – *The Modern Potter* by Ronald G. Cooper, 1947; George Wingfield Digby, 1952; and *The Work of the Modern Potter in England by Artist Potters in England* by Muriel Rose, 1955. These books give the marks of the famous English studio potters and illustrate typical examples of their wares. My *Encyclopaedia of British Pottery and Porcelain Marks* (Herbert Jenkins, 1964) will be found to contain references to some three hundred 20th-century studio potters working on their own account, most of whom have not before been made generally known. The collector who cannot, for example, afford the ruling prices for Bernard Leach's pots can certainly afford to purchase the equally individual work of his four sons, all of whom now have their own potteries and use their own marks. Here is one of many chances to get in on the ground floor of collecting. When next you want a fresh flower vase or fruit bowl, take a little trouble to find one made by an English studio potter rather than a cheap, gaudy, imported factory-made object. Museums should also show interest in the work of their local or home county potters and display their pots with a sequence of earlier wares.

TOY SERVICES

For at least two hundred years English potters have produced toy or miniature tea and dinner services as children's playthings. The early examples in salt glaze stoneware and tortoiseshell

34. Child's miniature dinner service in printed earthenware by Messrs Cockson & Harding *c.* 1858–62.   Tureen 3¾″ high.
Godden of Worthing Ltd.

glazed wares or the early porcelains are certainly outside the price range covered by this book. The 19th-century examples, however, are reasonably plentiful and individual units can be purchased at little cost.

These toy services are true miniatures of their full-size counterparts, both in form and pattern (see Plate 34) and a complete cross-section of, for example, 19th-century soup tureen forms can be displayed in a small hanging wall cabinet or in the space that two full-size tureens would require. Toy services, when complete, included all items that were in a full-size service so that a wide and interesting range of miniature wares of the 19th-century can be collected at little cost, indeed, few collectable wares can provide such diversity or take up so little space. Several examples will be found with maker's marks which can often be dated to narrow limits by the changes in the firm's

mark or title. As the collector proceeds he will be able to date his possessions approximately by their form or pattern.

Visitors to Queen Victoria's residence, Osborne House in the Isle of Wight, can see several toy services with which the Royal children played prior to 1862. Earlier in the century the Staffordshire potters exported many toy tea and dinner services to the United States of America; in the 1816–18 period it is recorded that blue printed toy teasets were sold in Boston for $1.10 a set, the equivalent of about 8s. Toy or miniature services, etc., in porcelain rather than earthenware are expensive and were made at the foremost factories – Spode, Swansea, Rockingham, etc.

CHAPTER EIGHT

VICTORIAN GLASS

FEW, IF ANY CLASS of antiques offer such scope to the collector of slender means as does Glass. Even today much 18th-century domestic glass can be purchased for under five pounds but undoubtedly the greatest opportunities lie in the study of 19th-century glass wares. Little research has been carried out, vast quantities exist and even documentary, museum examples can be purchased with little outlay. The following notes will therefore be restricted to 19th-century glass. The collector seeking information on earlier examples is well served by several reference books available in most public libraries.

PRESSED GLASS

I would like to concentrate on one aspect of Victorian glass, that produced by pressing. Pressed glass forms a large proportion of all glass produced in the 19th-century and although it is generally regarded with little favour, it can be very good. It is, of course, typical of the period and it was sold at a price that most people could afford.

A writer in the *Illustrated Encyclopaedia of the Great Exhibition of 1851* noted: 'By pressing into moulds, this elegant material is produced to the public in useful and symmetrical forms at prices considerably lower than those at which cut flint glass could possibly be offered. Many of the specimens of pressed glass exhibited have a degree of sharpness in all ornamental parts which renders it difficult, without close examination, to say whether or not they have been subjected to the glass-cutter's wheel.'

Many collectors find it difficult to distinguish between moulded and pressed glass. Various methods of *moulding* glass have been known for hundreds of years; several specimens of ancient glass formed by moulding exist and many examples of English 18th-century glass were partly formed in this manner. Decanters were often blown into a mould that roughly formed the decorative pattern, which in some cases, was then sharpened by the glass cutters working to the rough moulded design.

The pressing of glass is purely a 19th-century innovation. Opinions differ as to whether the method of pressing glass was first introduced in America or in England. An American, Deming Jarves, patented in December 1828 a method of 'pressing melted glass into moulds' and the American glass houses certainly produced more early pressed glass than did the English manufacturers. Trade reminiscences published in the magazine *Pottery Gazette* in the 1880s tell of the early English pressed wares and give the name of the die-sinker credited with making the first moulds. A contributor to the *Pottery Gazette* of August 1880 wrote:

We have good authority for stating that the first pressed tumbler was made in this country by Rice Harris, Birmingham, as far back as 1838. But some years earlier than this dishes had been pressed by Thomas Hawkes & Co. of Dudley and by Bacchus and Green of Birmingham. A few years before this dish period, America has the credit of pressing small plates and trifling matters . . . It would not be fair to omit the name of the first mould maker who made the tumbler in question – it was Mr James Stevens, then of Camden Street, Birmingham, and it is to him, and his sons, James and William, that the world is greatly indebted for the pressing of glass . . . Previous to this mould being made for tumblers, Mr James Stevens made some pressed salt moulds to order for an American gentleman visiting Birmingham. Mr Stevens was by trade a die-sinker.

A writer in the *Pottery Gazette* of August 1885 reports the difficulties encountered in the early experiments in making pressed glass tumblers, etc:

... Early pressed glass was made in thick topped goods, such as salt dishes, sweetmeats, and the like. The difficulty in pressing up the glass thin at the top was considered so impossible as to preclude the possibility of ever adopting the process to pressed tumblers as the metal (glass) chilled or set before it could press up. Molten glass cools very rapidly when in a small quantity ...

With *moulded* glass, the glass blower dips his blow pipe into the molten glass, then inserts the pipe and glass into a prepared mould and blows. This expands the glass like a bubble and as it does so it presses against the inside of the mould, taking the pattern. The mould, made in two or more sections, is then opened and the glass article finished in the normal manner.

The method used for pressing is different, and an understanding of the two techniques will help the collector to distinguish the moulded article from the pressed. The following account of pressing a tumbler was written by G.C.Mason in 1858 (*The Application of Art to Manufacturers*):

If it be required to give to the article any form or pattern unattainable by the simple means of blowing, etc., a mould is provided into which the glass is placed and, in this way, it receives the requisite impression as readily as wax. To form a tumbler in this way a mould of solid brass, about as large as a half-peck measure, and containing a hollow in it exactly of the form of a tumbler, is prepared. It has also a follower of brass of the same form, but so much smaller as to fit the inside of the tumbler. When the two parts are put together the space between them is of the exact thickness of the vessel required. In the process of manufacturing, three men and two boys are required. The first man dips an iron rod in the melted glass and moves it about until he has gathered a sufficient quantity of the fluid glass; he then holds it over the hollow of the mould and with a pair of shears cuts off what he judges to be just enough to constitute the tumbler. Instantly the next man brings down the follower with lever power and the melted glass is so compressed as to fill the cavity of the mould which he then turns bottom up, with a little blow, and the tumbler drops red-hot upon the stone table. One of the boys, with an iron rod having a little melted glass on its end, presses it on the bottom of the tumbler in the mouth of a glowing furnace, turns it rapidly till it is almost in a melted state, when it is passed to a third man, who whirls the rod and tumbler in a sort of arm-chair, at the same time removing all the roughness of the edge by means of a small iron tool. From him the rod passes to another boy, who separates from it the tumbler, which he places in the annealing oven. In this way these five hands will produce a beautiful tumbler in about forty-five seconds.

This contemporary account explains why the rough 'pontil mark' (the fracture resulting from the separation of the glass from the pontil rod, by which means it is handled), can occur on early pressed glass as well as on blown glass.

With moulded glass the walls of an article are of constant (or nearly equal) thickness, so that the design will appear in reverse inside, a convex curve on the outside being concave on the interior. With pressed glass the interior will be completely independent of the exterior design, as a separate metal plunger formed this, and the interior may also have a relief design of its own. Again, the pattern of a piece of pressed glass can be sharper than it is possible to acquire with blown moulded objects. Pressed glass, especially early examples, will show stress marks and straining – there is often a broken line or fault in the glass about a quarter of an inch below the rim. Both moulded and pressed glass will show mould marks, or slight raised lines where the different sections of the mould met. Moulded glass was often made up in sections, a moulded foot, for example, being added to a blown bowl, while pressed glass was normally made in one piece, with no additions. The object of pressing glass was of course to produce designs repeated on one piece after another with a minimum of labour, time and therefore expense.

Much pressed glass from the 1840s to the 1860s comprised low-priced utilitarian objects – tumblers, glasses, dishes, salts, etc., in clear glass, but later decorative articles in various coloured glasses were introduced. These were largely made at three North country glass houses. Fortunately the manufacturers often used a trade mark and registered some designs, so that their wares can be indentified and often dated.

The three leading manufacturers of this fancy pressed glass (often called 'slag', or 'end of the day' glass) were the Sowerby firm at Gateshead-on-Tyne, George Davidson & Co. of Gateshead and Greener & Co. of Sunderland. Before dealing with the products of these three firms, it would be as well to discuss the main type of 'slag' glass used in the manufacture of most of their wares. The general appearance of slag glass is similar to that of marble: it appears opaque and has marble-like streaks of lighter colour mixed with the darker main colour – often a deep purple.

The manufacture of this kind of semi-transclucent glass at Gateshead and Newcastle-upon-Tyne would appear to date back to at least the 1840s, for it was shown on the Newcastle stand at the Covent Garden Bazaar of 1845 and was then believed to be apparently unique. The *Art Union* magazine of April 1846 records a similar type of glass:

The imperfectly vitrified substance called Spelt which may be regarded as the middle term between glass and porcelain, appears to us likely to be found a very desirable addition to our decorative materials ... When the British Association met in Birmingham, a table was exhibited which had been manufactured at the glassworks near Gateshead, for the late Earl of Durham; the top was a slab of vitrified substance surpassing the richest jasper or porphyry in its

35. Sowerby's pressed glass bearing crest mark *c.* 1876–80.
    Diameter of plate 9½″.

36. Sowerby's pressed glass, a selection of designs registered between 1876 and 1880. Swan vase $4\frac{3}{4}''$.

colouring, and some smaller specimens were displayed in which the veining of the cat's eye, the cornelian and similar pebbles was most successfully imitated . . . The specimens which we have seen were so beautiful and so perfect, that we hope to find this branch of the glass making art rising rapidly both in use and estimation.

With few exceptions this type of glass did not 'catch on' until the 1870s and most examples of slag glass discussed and illustrated in this book were made between 1875 and 1890.

The name 'slag' is derived from the fact that slag, the waste material from the nearby iron blast furnaces, was mixed with the standard molten clear glass during the process of mixing. Alkalies and sand and other colouring matter, depending on the colour and quality of glass required, were added. A contemporary account written in 1880 makes it quite clear that this slag glass was prepared in a scientific manner, with fixed proportions of each material, and that the work of charging and withdrawing the liquid glass was continuous and proceeded from Monday morning until Saturday night. It would therefore seem that the term 'end of the day' glass, used by some collectors is a misplaced description, for it suggests that this glass was the result of mixing together the remains of various batches of glass left at the end of the day and forming with the resulting haphazard mixture the articles under discussion. This is far from the truth: the coloured glass was prepared to specifications and had to match the firm's various trade descriptions as mentioned in their catalogues. Apart from the marble-like veined glass, Sowerbys and other glass manufacturers were producing one colour, semi-opaque pressed glass wares in creams, greens, pinks, blues, browns and opaque white as well as pressed goods in clear glass. An American book *Milk Glass* by E. McCamly Belknap (1949) illustrates some English and American slag-type glass wares.

Undoubtedly the largest producers of coloured pressed glass were Messrs Sowerby of the Ellison Glass Works at Gateshead-on-Tyne. There had been several changes in title that can be summarized as follows:

George Sowerby c. 1824 to mid 1830s.
New Stourbridge Flint Glass Works mid 1830s to mid 1840s.
John Sowerby mid 1840s to c. 1854.
Sowerby and Neville c. 1855 to c. 1872.
Sowerby & Company c. 1872 to c. 1881.
Sowerby's Ellison Glass Works Ltd. December 1881 to present day.

The Sowerbys patented many improvements in glass machinery and in production methods.

A contemporary account published in the Newcastle Daily Chronicle of 21 October 1882 is of interest, as it shows the size and importance of the Sowerby factory:

. . . The Ellison Street Works are the largest pressed glass manufactory in the world. They cover an area of five and a half acres of ground, and from 700 to 1,000 hands are employed in them. They were established at Redheugh about a hundred years ago by the grandfather of the present managing partner, Mr J. W. Sowerby, but for very many years the entire operations of the factory have been conducted at Ellison Street. The production at the present time is about 150 tons per week of finished manufactured glass goods, and the materials necessary to make such an immense quantity of the substance may be said to be brought to Gateshead from the ends of the earth. The cryolite spar, used for the manufacture of opal glass, comes from Iceland; the nitre from Peru; the pearl ash from North America; the barytes from Germany; the manganese from Greece, and the fine silicous sand from Fontainbleau, in France. The soda, oxide of lead and arsenic used in the processes are, of course, obtained at home. The factory works continually day and night, all the year round; the hands employed being divided into three shifts of eight hours each. One hour of each shift may be deducted for meals, so that the workpeople labour for no more than seven hours per diem. The staple articles of production are drinking glasses of various kinds, decanters, salt cellars, cake and fruit dishes and plates, with various objects in opaque glass. To the production of these goods in the manufactory there is practically no limit but the demand, and the rate at which they can be turned out of hand may be guessed from the fact that each man working at the moulds can make from 1,100 to 1,200 tumblers during his seven hours work. In the melting room are nine furnaces containing in all 78 pots more or less constantly in use. Each pot holds from twelve to fifteen hundredweight of molten glass.

The Sowerby's Ellison Glass Works Ltd should not be confused with the separate company, Sowerby & Co., of the Lemington Glass Works, Newcastle-upon-Tyne. This latter firm was advertising in 1887 similar goods 'Pressed and Blown Glass of every kind in Flint and Colours, Cut and Engraved.' Their £4 sample package contained assorted Tumblers, Butters, Sugars and Creams, Sugars and Covers, Dishes, Plates, Bowls, Salts, Salvers and Sweets. These Lemington wares do not bear the crest mark which occurs on Sowerby's Ellison products.

The Sowerby Ellison pressed glass fancy goods are often of very attractive design and well finished. Many examples bear the peacock's head crest trade mark (see page 75) moulded in relief. It can look like a performing sea lion balancing an object on its head. The mark was registered in 1876 and can be found on the bottom of an object as well as in the interior; an interior mark is often missed on a quick inspection of a piece. As well as the crest mark, many specimens bear the diamond shaped design registration mark, from which the date of the *first* registration of the design can be ascertained (see page 24). The registered designs, some of which are illustrated in Plate 36, occur in the official files under Sowerby's name from 1875. A check list of their entries in the Design Registration files is given on page 75. A basic design can occur in several sizes of course in different coloured glasses. Selections of Sowerby's pressed glass are illustrated in Plates 35–37.

A report printed in the January 1880 issue of *Pottery Gazette* and written late in 1879 is interesting as it mentions the types of ware then in production.

Messrs Sowerby & Co., Ellison Glass Works, Gateshead-on-Tyne are making a speciality of their Patent Queen's Ivory Ware, (introduced in 1878) in entirely new designs, corresponding with carved Ivory examples. It is also made from original models by eminent artists, comprising Jardinieres, Rose baskets, Table decorations, Vases, Specimen vases, Toilet table requisites, Dessert ware, Tea cups and saucers, Tiles for cabinet work and Stoves, Card trays, &c. This well known firm are also manufacturing General Domestic Glass in Butters, Honeys, Sugars, Celeries, Biscuits, &c, in original and registered designs, Zephyr pressed tumblers and light elegant glass in great variety. They have a wide reputation for Vitro-Porcelain Dessert ware, Vases, &c., in turquoise and opal colours, Malachite, Agate and Sorpini in fancy vases, flower pots, &c.

Sowerby's did indeed have a wide reputation ; their wares were advertised 'for the markets of the world' and countries mentioned in advertisements of the 1880s include Belgium, Canada, Denmark, Germany, Holland, Italy, Norway, Sweden, Russia and the United States.

In 1880 George Sowerby visited America where he attempted to beat the Americans at their own game by selling his pressed glass half-pint tumblers at one shilling a dozen. The advertisements mention pattern books but none seems to have been preserved. Messrs Sowerby's Ellison Glass Works Ltd ceased advertising their fancy pressed coloured glass wares in the mid 1890s when apparently the demand for this novelty had ceased, after a period of popularity of twenty years. Judging by the number of designs registered, the peak years for this type of glass were 1877–9. A certain amount of blown 'Art Glass' was also produced in contrast to the mass-produced pressed wares. The company continues to the present day and produces clear glassware.

GREENER & CO.

Messrs H. Greener & Co. of the Wear Glass Works, Sunderland, were also large producers of fancy and useful wares in pressed glass. From *c*. 1858 to 1869 the firm was trading under the style of Angus and Greener; by July 1869 the name of Henry Greener was used alone. In 1881 Henry Greener was advertising 'Pressed and blown table Glass, cut and engraved, Flint and coloured, blue, green, amber, puce, blue and black, Majolica and Malachite – a large assortment always on hand of sugars and covers, butters and covers. plates, bowls and dishes suitable

for Exportation.' In 1883 'pressed glass in opal, brown-marble' is mentioned. By 1884 – and possibly before – Henry Greener had adopted his lion crest mark. In contemporary engravings of this mark, the lion is shown holding an axe but as the mark is very small when applied to glass the axe can very seldom be distinguished. A report in the Trade journal *Pottery Gazette* of January 1880 shows that Henry Greener was supplying the Canadian market and that special designs were made to commemorate special occasions. This quotation also mentions other Greener wares and types of glass:

Henry Greener, Wear Flint Glass Works, Millfield, Sunderland ... as an appropriate domestic memento of the attachment of all classes of our Canadian kinsmen to the Marquis of Lorne and the Princess Louise, has specially prepared some neatly designed Glass sugar basins and covers, creamer jugs, butter dishes and spoon holders. Each article is embellished with finely executed medallions, likenesses to Her Royal Highness and the Marquis, and an inscription containing the date of their landing at Halifax, N.S. There are also oval dishes in various sizes of a neat and suitable pattern. The sets are made in Flint Glass, Opal, Malachite and Blue or Black Majolica ...

Henry Greener had earlier worked with John Sowerby at Gateshead before joining James Angus at Sunderland. On the death of his partner, he built the large Wear Glass Works at Millfield, Sunderland. Henry Greener himself died in June 1882, aged sixty-two. For several years Greener's business had been running at a loss and in 1885 the works were taken over by James Jobling. Greener & Co.'s advertisements (see Plate 39) for pressed glass continue up to 1890 and the firm's name is listed at Sunderland until the 1920s although, as I have stated, the works were part of the present firm of James A. Jobling & Co. Ltd. Typical Greener pressed glass is illustrated in Plate 38.

GEORGE DAVIDSON & CO.

George Davidson & Co. of the Teams Glass Works, Gateshead-on-Tyne also made and marked with their turret and lion crest examples of slag type glass, but they are rarer than those made by Sowerby and by Greener. Davidson slag glass was produced mainly in the 1875–85 period, although George Davidson founded his glass works in 1867. This firm has recently re-introduced slag-type coloured glass.

By the late 1880s Davidson's were concentrating on a most attractive range of slightly tinted glass, shading upwards to an opal, pearl-like edge. The raised design may also show the opal colour in contrast to the translucent, coloured glass body. The trade name for this glass was 'Pearline'; the usual colour is a pale, attractive blue but other colours occur. The specimens of the glass which I have acquired do not bear the Davidson crest mark, but several shapes were registered and bear the moulded

TRADE MARK

1424

1398½

1388

1268

1407

1281

37. Sowerby advertisement of 1879 showing 'Patent Queen's Ivory Ware' and crest trade mark.

registration number. From this the date of registration and the maker can be ascertained. A selection of Davidson Pearline glass of the 1888–95 period is shown in Plate 40. These wares show the best qualities of glass, which is lost in the slag-type and other opaque glass. Displayed against light the Davidson 'Pearline' is most attractive.

Several other glass manufacturers made attractive pressed glass: W. H. Hepple & Co. of Newcastle-upon-Tyne registered some designs but their wares do not have a factory mark. Designs registered in the name of Molineaux, Webb & Co. of Manchester (an exhibitor at the 1851 Exhibition) often shows a frosted design contrasting with clear-polished glass. Another Manchester glass manufacturer, J. Derbyshire (& Son), produced attractive animal and figure subjects in clear, frosted or coloured glass. The glass made by J. Derbyshire often bears an anchor mark with the joined initials 'JD' which has in the past been incorrectly attributed to the Davenport firm of porcelain,

earthenware and glass manufacturers. Modern pressed glass ornaments in opal and coloured glass are now appearing on the market; some designs closely resemble Victorian designs.

A list of all the British makers of pressed glass would be both long and tedious, but their products are often very attractive and can be purchased at low cost. An interesting, informative collection could be made of examples bearing the diamond-shaped design registration mark, or of specimens bearing the firm's trade marks. Hugh Wakefield's *19th Century British Glass* (1961) is a useful reference book for the collector of Victorian glass.

The preceding notes have been concerned solely with one aspect of Victorian glass – that formed by pressing. Several other types offer similar scope and interest. The thousands of designs in etched or engraved glass are well worth the consideration of discerning collectors; the quality is often quite remarkable. The collector of engraved and acid etched glass will find a

38. Pressed glass bearing Messrs
Greener & Co's crest mark.
Lion ornament 6″ high.

study of John Northwood Junr's book on the career of his father, *John Northwood* (1958), most rewarding.

A good general reference book on our glass wares is *English Glass* (1935 and 1949) written by the Victoria and Albert Museum authority, W. A. Thorpe. I would especially recommend the following remarks quoted from the 1949 edition of this work:

At the present time the great opportunity for the small collector is a judicious sifting of Victorian glass. It is no use doing this in an eighteenth century or a twentieth century mood; one must feel and judge by Victorian standards. There is very good Victorian glass.

CREST MARKS

From left to right:

Sowerby & Co.; Greener & Co., on most specimens the lion faces left; George Davidson & Co.

CHECK LIST OF SOWERBY & CO'S ENTRIES IN THE PATENT OFFICE DESIGN REGISTRATION FILES 1872–83

Entries listed here under the *date of registration* can be checked against specimens by decoding the various letters and numerals in the diamond shaped registration marks on the object (see page 24) and then comparing the date and parcel number with the list. If they do not coincide the object was not registered by Sowerby & Co. between 1872 and 1883.

1872.	February 2	*Parcel no.*	1
	February 12		6
	February 29		5
	November 7		7
1873.	June 20		13
	July 31		5
1874.	January 15		6
	April 22		8
	June 1		8
	August 17		5
	September 10		6
1875.	January 1		2
	April 19		5
	June 5		9
	September 10		6
	October 28		4
	December 17		16
1876.	March 6		3

39. Greener & Co's 2007 pattern reproduced from an 1887 advertisement.

SUGAR, 2007.

BUTTER & COVER, 2007.

SUGAR, 2007A.

SHELL SWEET, 2007.

CREAM, 2007A.

PLATE, 2007.

SUGAR AND COVER, 2007A.

SUGAR AND COVER. 2007.

CREAM. 2007.

BISCUIT BOX, PLATE, & COVER, 2007.

40. Messrs Davidson's tinted pressed glass of the 1880's and 1890's. All specimens bear design registration numbers

March 9	*Parcel no.*	7
March 27		13
March 28		7
May 8		6
May 24		24
May 29		19
June 20		1
June 21		1
July 24		13
August 18		10
October 16		8
November 15		4

1877.	January 16	11
	February 13	8
	February 23	8
	March 1	5
	March 13	10
	March 15	1
	March 19	5
	March 22	12
	March 23	7
	March 29	4
	May 31	9
	September 18	7
	October 29	6
	November 20	4
	December 17	12
	December 19	1

1878.	February 20	3
	March 20	7
	March 22	8
	May 14	9
	June 25	10
	July 8	9
	July 29	4
	August 12	6
	August 16	11
	August 30	16
	November 4	10
	November 7	17
	November 20	11
	December 13	16
	December 23	2

1879.	January 8	*Parcel no.*	10
	February 8		8
	February 12		17
	March 10		9
	March 17		11
	April 28		7
	June 6		10
	June 30		14
	July 22		6
	July 29		13
	August 14		15
	September 4		7
	September 12		13
	September 18		13
	September 23		13
	December 2		21

1880.	January 9	11
	May 24	8
	July 13	11
	July 26	10
	September 14	1
	September 24	9

1881.	March 11	2
	March 19	11
	April 20	9
	May 19	9
	September 21	16
	December 14	6
	December 15	10

1882.	February 9	20
	April 28	13
	August 9	14
	August 29	13
	October 25	16

1883.	February 3	6

Many of these entries cover several different designs; that of 18 September 1877 relates to twenty-one designs. Several basic forms also occur with two or more different decorative motifs added, while all designs may be issued in different coloured glass.

CHAPTER NINE

GLASS FAIRY LIGHTS

COLOURED GLASS NIGHT, or 'Fairy' lights were extremely popular in the second half of the 19th-century and in the 1880s very many decorative fancy pieces were manufactured both in England and on the Continent. In recent years these objects have been avidly collected in America and at least two serious reference books have been written on the subject. Fairy lamps, which only a few years ago were merely novelties, now command several pounds and the more ornate examples are certainly outside the price range covered by this book.

At first the night lights were simple and utilitarian only. By 1886 Samuel Clarke had introduced his decorative 'Fairy' lamps and their use was extended from the illumination of nursery and bedroom to the enhancement of drawing and dining-rooms. A report of a fashionable dinner party in 1886 records their use as part of a table decoration as apparently a recent innovation:

... the new Fairy lights, which are well named, for their effect is quite fairy-like. They are small lights, which are placed in the centre of a circular flower vase, and each is covered with a tinted glass shade, some opal, some pale rose, some of the tenderest of soft green. The flower circle was filled with moss and ferns, with just two or three pink and yellow tulip buds in each. The softness of the light gave an added beauty to the flowers and ferns, and as the fairy lamps are quite low on the table, the effect was extremely becoming to the diners ...

The illustrations of Fairy lamps of this type in Plates 41 are reproduced from Clarke's advertisements of 1886. Several other contemporary quotations relating to Fairy lamps may be found in journals of the 1885–90 period, a selection from which is quoted later in this chapter. A most interesting reference was quoted in "The World" of 21 April 1886, describing the types of Fairy lamp then in use:

There are new developments now in the modes of using the Fairy lights which will be sure to make them very popular this season. Chandeliers from five to eighty lights, in all kinds of pretty glass, are made now and, with these and wall brackets, it is possible to illuminate a large dining-room most successfully. The dome-shaped glasses look very well, some in mother o'pearl, some in stained glass, in cameo or in striped glass. One struck me as particularly pretty, made in a very soft pale green colour. Of course, these coloured glasses to a certain extent obscure the light, and in a short time some shades of richly cut glass will be ready which will quite double the light instead of rendering it dimmer.

For ball-rooms, these lights are really perfection, as nothing can happen to them, no draught affects them in the least, no grease can fall, they create no heat, the light is always steady, and has the curious advantage of increasing in brilliance as it burns. Pretty little hanging lamps are made for conservatories or gardens, suspended by a slender chain, so that they can be put right among the flowers, and also lamps with spikes for illuminating flower beds.

The name Clark was associated with night lights from the early part of the Victorian era. George Miller Clarke took out a patent in 1844 for an improvement in night lights, and in 1857, Samuel Clarke took out a patent relating to this form of illumination. It is Samuel Clarke's name which will always be associated with decorative Fairy lamps. He was primarily a manufacturer of high grade candles, tapers, etc., and did not himself manufacture the glass and ceramic holders and their shades which today are the concern of collectors; he did, however, perfect and publicize the objects on a massive international scale. The wax lights were made of a pure, clear and steady-burning wax, with none of the unpleasant odour of oil, or tallow candles. The double wick (which was of rush, not cotton) was twisted in such a manner that it partly unwound as the wax slowly melted and so gave a large oval flame (these wicks should never be touched or trimmed). The squat circular lights burned for various periods, ranging from four to eleven hours. Many Fairy lamps will be found with their 'wax candles' still in place.

Samuel Clarke spent vast sums in advertising his various types

41. Samuel Clarke's 'Fairy' lamp flower holders etc. Reproduced from an 1886 advertisement.

of candle lights; in the 1880s he also enjoyed widespread free publicity in most magazines of his day. The specimens advertised were intended for a variety of uses and the price of objects listed ranged from chandeliers of one hundred and ten lights at £105 each to simple lights at 6d. each. Other firms such as Sowerby's, Ellison of Gateshead-on-Tyne supplied utilitarian examples at 2s. a dozen, 'reductions for quantities'. One of Samuel Clarke's successful advertising schemes was carried out in 1886 when he supplied free of charge 'many thousands' of his 'Fairy' lamps to the Royal Botanic Society for their Summer Fêtes. The publicity this offered resulted in the sale of thousands of Fairy lamps for garden use. In the following year nearly twenty thousand Clarke lamps were hung in the trees, arranged in the flower beds or used to illuminate the covered walks of the Society's grounds. A contemporary account records that the illuminations were perfect – 'all sweetness and light'. Indoors, Clarke's lights were used in conjuction with specially designed candlesticks and ornamental candelabra in porcelain, glass, silver plate or brass. Some of the finest porcelain bases were made by the Royal Worcester Company.

Various trade names will be found on Fairy lamps; an early Clarke name for his candles was 'Pyramid'. In January 1887 the name 'Fairy-Pyramid' was registered, these were smaller than the original 'Fairy' lamp. A smaller lamp still, named 'Wee Fairy' was introduced in October 1887. The Clarke fairy trade mark occurs moulded in the base of the candle container (not normally on the ornamental base, into which the container fitted). On early examples the fairy's left hand is close to her head. The name 'Cricklight' occurs on many specimens made after 1895; the name was derived from Cricklewood in North West London where the Clarke factory was then situated.

Other trade names were used by manufacturers who sought to emulate Clarke's success in the Fairy lamp trade. 'Glow-worm' was used by J. Walsh, Walsh of Birmingham from 1887. Edward Webb of the White House Glass Works, Wordsley produced attractive night lights and flower bowls in several styles and in twelve 'charming colours' under the trade name 'Will o' the Wisp'. 'Bijou' was a name used by the importers J. Stembridge & Co. of London (see advertisement, Plate 45); this firm also introduced in 1889 a tall lighthouse night-light flower-stand, which was made in clear glass, in amber or in blue glass.

Probably the most expensive form of decoration is that known as Burmese: the semi-opaque salmon pink glass is shaded into a lemon-yellow, like 'the dawn of another day'. The treatment was patented in America by the Mount Washington Glass Co. of New Bedford, Mass. on 16 December 1885. This delicately blended glass (aided by good publicity), quickly caught the public's fancy; the English rights were acquired by Thomas Webb & Sons who then manufactured it under the name 'Queen's Burmese' from September 1886. Night lights and many other articles may be found with acid engraved marks incorporating this name and that of Thomas Webb & Sons. Some specimens of Burmese lights are also decorated with slight painted floral sprays, etc. A trade report, late in 1887, records the fact that:

The Queen's Burmese ware continues to enjoy great popularity, and orders which are received for articles made of the ware afford Messrs Webb no lack of employment, indeed in this department they are as busy as they can possibly be . . .

The collector will have to be lucky to find marked examples at a price below five pounds but one of the joys of collecting night-lights is that long forgotten caches may be discovered in the most unexpected places, for the fashion was short-lived; examples were put away by one generation and forgotten by the next. Old house sales will often yield boxes of Fairy lamps tucked away in an attic. I once discovered a hamper full of Clarke's lights, each packed in its original box, with instructions, wax candle, coloured-glass base and shade.

The demand for 'Fairy'-type lights was an international one. Many Continental manufacturers produced examples and even advertised in English trade papers. Samuel Clarke's wares were patented, presumably with good reason, in France, Belgium, Germany, Austria, Spain, Russia, Australia and the United States where he also had agents. Glass works in America, too, produced decorative night-lights.

To keep the demand brisk, the manufacturers had to introduce new colours and novelties at frequent intervals. It is this fact that gives the present day collector vast scope for the formation of his collection. The Clarke advertisements repro-

42. Clarke's advertisement of 1891 showing rare decorative jewelled Christmas tree and peacock shades. These were made in Austria.

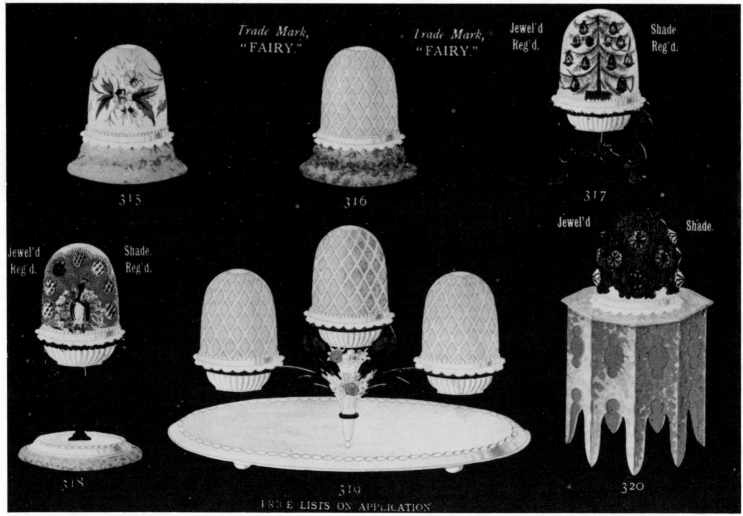

FREE LISTS ON APPLICATION

duced in Plates 41–43 will give an idea of the different models in production. The collector will soon become aware of the wonderful colour effects that are not apparent from these black and white photographs (the original advertisements are in colour) but some of the names will give an indication of the colour ranges – Nacre de Perle, Citron Satin, Rose Cleveland, Amber Tinted Satin, Ruby Threaded Opal, etc. The term 'Cleveland' was used to describe different coloured vertical bands which were sometimes twisted so that spirals were formed. The term 'satin' was used to describe a most pleasing form of acid treated surface with a warm satin-like finish. Quilted satin shows an attractive crisscross pattern in the glass. The specimens shown in Plate 41 are of pulled thread ware, the threaded lines being pulled upwards to form a draped effect. Many different varieties of threaded glass lamps were made. Some domes are plain, others are ribbed or have other decorative forms.

The collector of statistics may like to know the original prices of the main types of Clarke Fairy lamps.

The following list shows the wholesale prices in 1889 of the various standard designs, arranged in ascending order of price:

Clear glass or opal shades.	6s. a dozen
Garden lamp shades in Blue, Green, Amber or Opalescent.	6s. a dozen
Garden lamp shades in Ruby.	8s. a dozen
'Fairy' Shades, 'Cleveland' types.	9s. a dozen
'Fairy' Shades, 'Satin' type.	9s. a dozen
'Fairy' Shades, 'Threaded' types.	9s. a dozen
'Fairy' Shades, 'Parian' in Rose, Citron and Cleveland.	9s. a dozen
'Fairy' Shades, 'Verre Moire' types.	12s. a dozen
'Fairy' Shades, 'Silk Finish'.	12s. a dozen
'Fairy' Shades, Ruby, plain or twisted, clear or obscured.	12s. a dozen
'Fairy' Shades, 'Burmese' undecorated	12s. a dozen
'Fairy' Shades, 'Corallo' in Blue, Brown or Yellow.	16s. a dozen
'Fairy' Shades, Transparent porcelain, undecorated.	16s. a dozen
'Fairy' Shades, 'Silk finish'.	18s. a dozen
'Fairy' Shades, Crinkled top.	18s. a dozen
'Fairy' Shades, Transparent porcelain, decorated.	24s. a dozen
'Fairy' Shades, Burmese, decorated.	30s. a dozen
'Fairy' Shades, Cameo shades.	36s. a dozen

In 1910 Messrs Price's Patent Candle Co. Ltd, an old established firm of international repute (employing seven hundred people in 1849) purchased the Clarke concern but for many years the new management retained and used Clarke's name and trade marks on night-light holders. This firm are still operating in London and are the world's largest producers of candles.

The collector seeking a different approach could form an interesting collection of novelty shades, such as those shown in Plate 44. As a general rule, these were produced by the smaller firms rather than by Clarkes. Other regular shades can be found on unusual bases, often in decorated china instead of glass. Night-light-type candles were also used to heat the collectable and decorative china heaters of food or liquids (termed Veilleuses) but these are outside the scope of the present book.

43. Floral 'Fairy' lamps of various designs. These shades were of foreign make imported and sold by Samuel Clarke. *c.* 1892.

I would like to think that the collector of decorative night-lights did not keep his purchases locked in a display cabinet, but that on suitable occasions they graced the table and were used as they were originally intended. The effect of these table ornaments can be quite beautiful. Replacement 'candles' can still be obtained but care must be taken to ensure that the light is placed exactly in the centre of the base, so that the main heat escapes straight through the central vent and does not heat one side of the shade causing it to crack. The amateur electrician may wish to light his collection, whether it is in a case or on the table, by means of low-powered light bulbs, such as are used on a Christmas tree.

The collector will no doubt progress as opportunity and his pocket permits to the more elaborate rarities, epergnes (sometimes on mirror bases), chandeliers, mirrors, etc. Related objects include lithophane shades (see Chapter 4) and coloured animal-head shades, probably intended for nursery use. These can be very amusing and some specimens bear pattern registration numbers of the 1883–90 period. Much interesting information will be found in Amelia E. MacSwiggan's 'Fairy Lamps, Evening's Glow of Yesteryear' (1962,

Fountainhead Publishers, New York) and in Dorothy Tibbett's 'Clarke's Fairy Lamps' (1951 Mission Press, Huntington Press, U.S.A.).

The price of night-lights has risen to a great extent in recent years and as the available hidden reserves are found this trend will be accentuated. The prospective collector will be well advised to start collecting Fairy lights without delay. I am informed that in America the price and scarcity of examples has resulted in reproductions being placed on the market.

CONTEMPORARY REFERENCES TO CLARKE'S 'FAIRY' LAMPS AND IMITATIONS

The first reference to Samuel Clarke's 'Fairy' lamps occurs in the Trade magazine *Pottery Gazette* of February 1886. Mr Clarke's name is not mentioned although his trade name for the lamps, 'Fairy', is given, and, in an article which forms a sequel in the next issue, it is made quite clear that both references relate to Clarke's lamps. This notice of February is very impor-

44. Five novel night lights of which many were produced in the late 1880's and early 1890's. *Godden of Worthing Ltd.*

tant as it reveals the manufacturers of the first lamps, Messrs Stuart & Sons of the Red House Glass Works, Stourbridge, and also indicates that this was the first time that the trade writer had seen such novelties. This hitherto unrecorded notice reads:

Messrs Stuart & Sons of the Red Glass Works, Stourbridge, have removed their London show-rooms to St Andrews Buildings, Holborn Circus . . . Their opening day was on the 26th prox. They had a fine display of rich table and fancy glass. A very pretty and taking novelty was a coloured flower vase with growing ferns, in the centre of which is placed a 'Fairy-light' lamp, showing through an ornamental coloured glass shade; this, burning in the middle of the green leaves, has a very pretty effect. We should think that a few placed at night in a shop window would prove an attractive draw.

In the following issue of March 1886 the subject of **Fairy** lamps is continued:

We referred very briefly in our last issue to the 'Fairy' lamps and 'Fairy' lights which have recently been patented and introduced by Mr Samuel Clarke, Child's Hill, London N.W. These are glass shades of various colours for burning underneath them candle lights with double wicks, which throw out a beautiful soft steady light. Two of these we illustrate, but they do but scant justice to the large variety of forms in which they are being adapted. For ornamentally lighting drawing and ball-rooms, conservatories, evening fetes, table decorations, &c., when surrounded with ferns and flowers they have an exceedingly pretty effect. Several large City china shops, acting on our suggestion, have made good use of them during the last month (February 1886) in making effective window displays. The shades we may mention are of Stourbridge manufacture, and some pretty colours and combinations have been produced for the purpose. We congratulate Mr Samuel Clarke on bringing out one of the happiest novelties in the trade we have seen for some time.

The first non-trade account of the newly introduced 'Fairy' lamp is given in the magazine *Truth* of 25 February 1886, and these comments are quoted at the beginning of the chapter.

A review in *The World* of 21 April 1886 is interesting as it lists some of the earliest styles and colours; this has been quoted on page 78.

Several contemporary notices record the introduction of new styles and colours. One from *The Ironmonger* of 11 September 1886 speaks of the recent introduction of 'richly cut glass shades' as opposed to the earlier plain or fluted types. (The first cut

45. 'Bijou' Fairy type lamps imported and sold by J. Stembridge & Co of London. Reproduced from an 1888 advertisement.

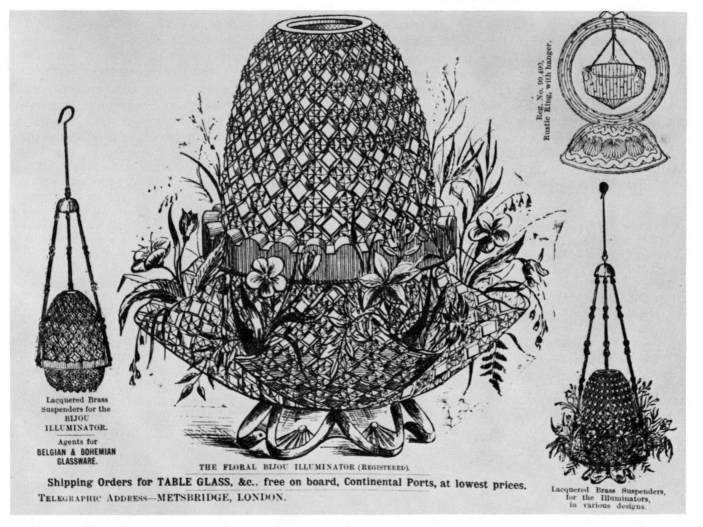

Reg. No. 99,492,
Rustic Ring, with hanger.

Lacquered Brass
Suspenders for the
BIJOU
ILLUMINATOR.

Agents for
BELGIAN & BOHEMIAN
GLASSWARE.

THE FLORAL BIJOU ILLUMINATOR (REGISTERED).

Shipping Orders for **TABLE GLASS**, &c., free on board, Continental Ports, at lowest prices.

TELEGRAPHIC ADDRESS—METSBRIDGE, LONDON.

Lacquered Brass Suspenders,
for the Illuminators,
in various designs.

pattern is no. 76 in the illustrated catalogue and was issued in July or August 1886.) The reference reads:

Mr Samuel Clarke, Ely Place, E.C. and Child's Hill, N.W. is continuously introducing new and pretty designs in the 'Fairy' lamp department, the expectations of a heavy demand for these specialities being supported by the favour which Colonial and foreign visitors have bestowed upon them. 'Fairy' lamp pendants and cluster lights on stands, grouped in the most charming manner, with shades of exquisite hue, give an idea how attractive this style of illumination can be made, and the skilful taste of the manufacturer has been developed in this direction in a marvellous degree. Quite recently a number of richly cut glass shades have been introduced, and the prismatic colours blended with floral decorations have all been introduced as a tribute to the 'Fairy' lamp, and the splendid success which followed the efforts thus put forth is another proof that a dainty thing in good taste will be sure to make its way, even with an unpromising beginning, but when handled in the practical manner as the 'Fairy' lamps have been, the reward is proportionately greater.

Probably the most important contemporary reference concerns the introduction of the very popular 'Queen's Burmese' glass shades made for Samuel Clarke by Thomas Webb & Sons under an American patented process (taken out by the Mount Washington Glass Co. on 16 December 1885). As will be seen the first 'Burmese' glass night-lights were shown to the trade in January 1887 (the first 'Burmese' lamp in Clarke's pattern book is no. 138), although other examples in this type of shaded glass were probably introduced by Thomas Webb a few months before this, as the trade mark found on such wares was entered at the Patent Office in September 1886. It was the undoubted success of Webb's 'Burmese' glass wares that prompted Clarke to have shades and other fittings made in the same material. Contemporary price lists show that the Burmese wares were expensive compared with other types and the collector will find that this still holds true today. The account which follows was written in December 1886 and appeared in the *Pottery Gazette* of January 1887:

Queen's Burmese ware is of the nature of glass, its discovery (for that it was rather than an invention) is due to the United States; the ware is now manufactured in England under a patent. Its loveliness when illuminated is due to the material, its translucency and its blending from a flesh pink to yellow, which is of the perfectness that radiated heat alone can effect.

The Patentee of the 'Fairy' lights considering the Burmese ware very suitable for his 'Fairy' lamps has had made of that ware some very beautiful designed Chandeliers, Candelabra, Brackets, Bowls, &c., which he is pleased to add to his already large and varied stock of 'Fairy' lamps.

His additional Show-rooms at 31, Ely Place, Holborn Circus are fitted up extensively for the display of these beautiful Goods and will be ready for inspection by the Trade on Friday, the 7th of January

1887 on which day there will be a Special Illuminated display . . .

A reference to a 'Burmese' glass chandelier of sixty-eight lights occurs in the February 1887 issue of *Pottery Gazette*:

Mr Samuel Clarke has just completed, at 31, Ely Place, Holborn E.C. his display of 'Burmese Fairy' lights. A beautiful 68 light chandelier, made by Thomas Webb & Sons, is a perfect masterpiece of glass manufacturing and all who wish to see the capabilities of the English trade should not fail to see this distinct success. The Burmese glass, as already explained, is produced by a patent process, and the ruby top gradually merging into the white is an effect in the complete chandelier which quite baffles description. The art metal work adds beauty to the whole and the minor parts and flower holders have been executed with artistic skill of high merit. The whole forms a superb chandelier, and in a large drawing or ball-room would produce a sensation for a whole season.

There are other adaptations of the 'Burmese Fairy' lamps arranged for three lights upwards and cut glass chandeliers and table lamps in a variety of patterns . . .

While most designs enjoyed a short lived popularity, the 'Burmese' shades continued in favour for several years, as can be seen by the following notice which appeared in the *Pottery Gazette* of March 1889:

The 'Burmese' ware introduced by Messrs Thomas Webb & Sons, Dennis Works, Stourbridge, a couple of years ago continues as popular as ever . . . During the winter Fairy lights in this ware met with a large sale and the difficulty was to manufacture them with sufficient rapidity. Fairy lights have been made in endless varieties in glass; but none have been found so popular as the Burmese ware . . .

A further notice in the November 1890 issue of the same periodical shows that there was no decline in the popularity in these 'Burmese' objects nearly four years after the first mention of them; it also contains references to jewelled and floral shades:

Mr Samuel Clarke of Cricklewood, London is still bringing out fresh novelties in his world-renowned Fairy Lamps. It is wonderful the amount of ingenuity and art brought to bear upon these fairy light objects. We visited the show-rooms the other day at 31, Ely Place, Holborn, where rich chandeliers in Burmese glass, cut glass candelabra, painted and cut and engraved mirrors fit to grace a Nabob's palace were to be seen. Some of the chandeliers run into hundreds of pounds, which will give our readers some idea of the graceful grouping of the lamps and the combination of artistic glass and brass work . . .

In ordinary Fairy lights for table decorations, there are all kinds of shapes and sizes, for all sorts of conditions of mankind. What are chiefly selling at the present time are the two extremes – either expensive and good ones, or else cheap low-priced ones. Some of the shades are jewelled with coloured glass, and the Burmese is still a favourite. The illustration below [a flower-shaped shade see Plate 43] is one of his latest ideas – the new 'Floral' lamp. On a stand of golden brown plush rises a dainty little structure in the form of a full blown rose.

The curled petals are of the palest rose pink glass, delicately veined, the inner ones being of a deeper tint . . . Mr Clarke, with business-like judgement, has entered into an arrangement with Messrs Gordon & Co. to have his lamp placed in every bedroom in their hotels, with a request for the visitors to use them at night instead of gas, which they deem unhealthy and dangerous. When we consider the hundreds of bedrooms and the wealthy class of visitors using such hotels as the Metropole (London), the Grand and Metropole (Brighton) and the new hotel just opened at Monte Carlo, the privilege allowed is a good stroke of business on his part, and will no doubt be the means of extending their sale in this direction.

As may be expected Samuel Clarke was quick to introduce special designs, one popular example having the shade formed as a crown. Such objects were well fitted to mark the Queen's Jubilee of 1887 and 1897. Several magazines of the period referred to Clarke's Jubilee lamps.

A reference to new designs introduced late in 1891 is contained in the *Pottery Gazette* of January 1892:

Among the fancy stocks this season may be seen the latest novelty in jewelled fairy lamps. An opaque lamp has holes drilled in it, in which are inserted vari-coloured glass diamonds. One has a Christmas-tree painted on in raised enamel, the jewels lighting up the tree after the manner of the old fashioned coloured candles. Then we have another pattern bearing a painted peacock. The eyes of his tail feathers sparkle and glitter with coloured diamond-like brilliancy. The effect produced is simply charming. See Plate 42.

However, at this period, the extent of Samuel Clarke's advertising diminishes and, reading between the lines of several notices, we gain the impression that the 'Fairy' lamp trade is fast coming to an end. Not only had the novelty worn off after seven years but electric light was rapidly gaining favour for lighting the ballrooms and dining-rooms which had been the intended home of most of the ornate, decorative and relatively expensive Fairy lamp novelties introduced between 1886 and 1892.

Clarke had strong competition from other manufacturers, both English and Continental, and prices had to be cut to meet this. A notice to the trade issued in the middle of 1887 draws attention to the new reduced prices (coloured 'Fairy-Pyramids' in box with light at 2d. each) and ends with the announcement, 'The Trade are again cautioned not to stock largely as IF NECESSARY the prices will again be reduced.'

Little has been written of the work of Clarke's competitors. Some very fine coloured and cut glass lamps with flower-holders were registered and made by Edward Webb of the White House Glass Works, Stourbridge. Twelve of these designs were advertised in November 1886.

That Samuel Clarke was troubled by imitators as early as 1886 can be seen from the following apology, dated 4 January 1887, which he had published with several others in the same year:

Sir, On the 25th November last (1886) a person of the name of Cottrell sent to my establishment an order for a 7/6 'Fairy' lamp. Not having one in stock, one of my assistants, without my knowledge, sent off a lamp (something like your 'Fairy' lamp) supplied to me by Messrs Blumberg & Co., but not bearing your Trade Mark 'Fairy' and invoiced it as 'Fairy' lamp, of which you complain as an infringement of your Registered Trade Mark . . .

Messrs Blumberg & Co. sold a very large range of imported and English china, glasswares, lamps and jewellery. Clarke's later advertisements were continually warning the public against imitations of his 'Fairy' lamp.

Early in 1887 the wholesale firm of F.B.Bach & Co. was advertising 'Registered China Floral Shades for Fairy Lights'. They took the form of roses in red, yellow, pink, pink tinted, yellow tinted and white, and tulip. Tulip shades were made in pink and in yellow. The designs were registered in 1886 and the shades made by Pillivuyt & Co. of Limoges, France; they are most effective. Samuel Clarke also issued floral shades and, as late as 1891, Messrs Walsh, Walsh of Birmingham issued floral type lamps which 'created quite a revival in the use of Fairy lights as a decoration'.

The wholesale and export firm of J. Stembridge & Co. (agents for Belgian and Bohemian glass) of Red Lion Square, London, registered a cut glass 'Bijou Illuminator' in 1888; it was issued in several different styles, as can be seen by the contemporary advertisement, Plate 15. (The simple cut shades and bases were sold wholesale at 4s. 6d. a dozen.) At the same time this firm advertised imported 'Bijou Transparencies – The latest Novelties in illuminators'. These 'Fairy'-like lamps and novelties were made of porcelain (usually unglazed), the shades or panels were of the lithophane type (see Chapter 4 and plate 15) and were lit and brought to life by the night-light inside. It is interesting to see that, as late as 1888, lithophane lamps were described as 'the latest novelties'.

Simple glass shades and bowls were being advertised under the name 'Glow-worm' in 1888 and 1889. This trade name was registered by the glass manufacturers J. Walsh, Walsh of Birmingham in 1887. In 1888 Sowerbys Ellison Glass Works Ltd of Gateshead-on-Tyne, pressed glass manufacturers, introduced 'The new "Ellison" dinner lamp, to burn Clarke's "Pyramid" light. Price 2/- per dozen, reduction for quantities.'

In 1889 J. Walsh, Walsh brought out a small inexpensive glass lamp, the stem of which was shaped like a palm tree, with shades in pink, blue or yellow glass, with small drops. The trade announcement stated: 'This is a vast improvement on the Fairy lamps. The effect is quite fairy-like but giving a stronger light . . .'

Some attractive china shades were made in porcelain and take the form of the heads of animals or birds. A contemporary trade notice which appeared in November 1889 mentions these objects as recent innovations (the owl shade was registered in 1889).

The Cat lamps and Owl night-lights, weird looking as they are, seem to have hit the taste of the public. They are being largely employed for attracting the notice of passers-by, calling special attention to novelties, filling up odd nooks, and dark corners, and for enhancing the beauty and attractiveness of table decorations . . .

Before closing this chapter on 'Fairy' lamps and similar objects the subject of Samuel Clarke's 'Cricklights' must be touched upon. These are similar to 'Fairy' lights in that they consist of a glass container and shade intended to hold candles of the night-light variety but the shade is made of clear, uncut glass of graceful shape. The name 'Cricklight' is moulded into the base and often occurs on the shade or its metal fitting. They were mainly intended to fit into candlesticks, candelabra, etc., and the bases often have glass pegs so that they could be placed in the holders at will. The Royal Worcester Porcelain Company Ltd supplied some fine figure and vase bases for use with Cricklight fittings. The clear shades ensured greater light than had been possible with the early coloured glass 'Fairy' lamp shades.

The trade name 'Cricklight' was registered in 1889 – as the fairy lamps went out of vogue in the early 1890s, the new Cricklights took their place as a mode of lighting a dining-table. With the greater light and decorative high standard bases they were better able to compete with electric light. They were made over a long period and catalogues were issued as late as 1931. The column bases for candelabra were made in brass, silver plate and in fine quality cut glass of many different patterns. Such important pieces are, of course, outside the price range covered in this book but they are related to 'Fairy' lamps and the collector of the latter will probably wish to graduate to Cricklights to complete his collection. Cricklights were not issued with fancy coloured shades, but some examples have subsequently been fitted with 'Fairy' shades, with good effect.

Samuel Clarke's 'Fairy' Trade Mark

Clarke's Registered Trade names and Trade marks

Date of application 18/1/76. Hand lamp with 'Pyramid' candle.
      ,,   ,,   ,,   14/9/80. Trade name 'Pyramid' used 20 years before January 1876 (other applications note that this name had been used since 1860).
Date of application 4/1/84. Trade name 'Burglar's Horror'.
      ,,   ,,   ,,   21/4/85. Trade name 'Fairy' (name only).
      ,,   ,,   ,,   1/12/86. Trade *Mark* of fairy with wand.
      ,,   ,,   ,,   20/1/87. Trade name 'Fairy-Pyramid'.
      ,,   ,,   ,,   10/10/87. Trade name 'Wee Fairy'.
      ,,   ,,   ,,   25/6/89. Trade name 'Cricklite'.
The 'Queen's' Burmese Ware. Thomas Webb & Sons' Trade Mark was entered in September 1886.

CHAPTER TEN

GLASS PAPERWEIGHTS

IT WILL NO doubt surprise many readers that the subject of Glass Paperweights has been included in this book, for press reports frequently publicize the fact that hundreds of pounds are willingly given for specimens. A sale held by Messrs Sotheby & Co. in March 1965 was devoted solely to glass paperweights and the prices ranged from the cheapest at three pounds to three thousand three hundred pounds, giving an average price of slightly over two hundred and twenty pounds.

These high prices are paid for fine early specimens made in France, England, America and other countries in the 1840s. The best specimens are attributed to the French glass houses. The decorative motifs are modelled in coloured glass and are encased within the clear glass. Many fine floral patterns (called 'millefiori') were formed of tiny coloured canes.

These specimens are most decorative and have been extensively copied both in England and on the Continent. A pre-war English firm advertised:

Daisy pattern paperweights. Dated 1848. Diameter 3″. 25/- each.

Similar floral paperweights are still made today and some of these are 'aged' and sold as antique.

It is not the purpose of this book to recommend that the new collector should seek inferior copies of expensive wares. He should instead turn his attention to a class of ware that is neglected but still of decorative and other interest, and typical of its period – not a mere copy of an earlier style. Such a field exists in the thousands of relatively inexpensive Victorian scenic paperweights that depict famous resorts and local places of interest (see Plates 46–7.) These are most colourful and interesting, especially the street scenes with Victorian costume, coaches, etc.

These weights seem to have enjoyed widespread appeal; examples may be found with titles in European languages and others depict American views – The White House; Worlds Columbian Exposition 1893, etc.

The scenic glass paperweights were made both in England and on the Continent and were sold in stationers' and other shops catering for the tourist. I have traced two references to these in novels; the first occurs in Emile Zola's 'Nana', published in France in 1880:

..., So to escape from their curiosity, he went and stood in front of a stationer's window, where he inspected, apparently with profound attention, a display of glass paperweights, containing coloured representations of landscapes ...

A later reference occurs in Arnold Bennett's 'The Card', first published in 1911:

... mixed up with papers and sixpenny novels on the bookstall were a number of souvenirs of Llandudno – paper knives, pens, paperweights, watch cases, pen cases, all in light wood or glass and ornamented with coloured views of Llandudno ... Ruth remembered that she had even intended to buy a crystal paperweight with a view of the Great Orme at the bottom. The bookstall clerk had several crystal paperweights with views of the pier, the Hotel Majestic, the Esplanade, The Happy Valley, but none of the Great Orme ...

This type of scenic paperweight, in which the coloured print was affixed to the bottom of the glass weight, the dome shape of which acted as a magnifying glass, was certainly invented by 1851, and some specimens may well be of the same period (the late 1840s) as the floral paperweights that command hundreds of pounds. I have before me two scenic paperweights showing views of the 1851 Exhibition building – The Crystal Palace, in Hyde Park. One of these Exhibition views was registered at the Patent Office in October 1851 in the name of Messrs Berns, Blumberg & Co. of St Pauls Church Yard. Six other designs featuring the exhibition were registered by George Novra, of London.

The early examples display coloured printed views, some of which had small pieces of tinsel inserted behind windows to give a realistic glass-like effect. The later paperweights from about the 1890s were based on photographic views and are, as a general rule, not nearly as colourful as the mid-Victorian examples. The weights of the 1850–70 period are of a plain circular outline with the domed top no more than an inch and a quarter high. After about 1870 many fancy shapes (hearts, etc.) were introduced, some of which incorporate pressed fancy borders to the pictures.

I have had the greatest difficulty in collecting material on the manufacturers of these articles. None of the English glass firms owned up to making specimens, and it was only when my investigations were aimed at the selling outlets rather than the manufacturing side that some information was forthcoming. The Editor of *The Stationer* kindly allowed me to appeal for information in this trade journal. The only helpful reply came from Messrs F. Frith & Co. Ltd, Publishers and Printers of Reigate, Surrey. Although the date is later than that which really concerns us, the mystery of why the English glass manufacturers were unable to supply information is explained. The letter reads in part:

We note with interest that you are looking for information with regard to glass paperweights. We ourselves manufactured many thousands of these prior to 1937. The glass used to be imported from Belgium, and we used to print and stick on the appropriate pictures. . . .

The Continental connection with these seemingly very Eng-

46. Three typical Victorian paperweights, some of which depict foreign scenes.

lish view paperweights is confirmed by interesting correspondence with a now retired stationer, Mr Percy Lapworth, of Arundel, Sussex. This was a result of following up one of his paper labels which I found still affixed to the base of a local view paperweight. Writing of the period 1900–14 Mr Lapworth relates that the paperweights were made in Germany and that an agent toured the country taking orders and collecting local views (taken from picture postcards) as required by the retailer. These he then took over to Germany and the resulting paperweights arrived back in time for the summer season. Mr Lapworth mentions the then current retail prices of 9d., 1s., 1s. 3d. and 1s. 6d. according to size and shape. Many late photographic paperweights have a reference number after the title – 'West Parade, Bognor 36492 JY', for example.

Having written the above remarks relating to the foreign provenance of most such paperweights I found, while looking for other objects, a clear illustration of one in a British manufacturer's catalogue – John Ford's catalogue of *c.* 1868. Ford worked the Holyrood Flint Glass Works at Edinburgh; an oval weight is illustrated, the scene being of Burns' Monument and Arthur's Seat, Edinburgh. There is also the caption 'Letter-weights, Edinburgh Views – 9s., 13s. 6d., 17s. 6d., 22s. 6d. a dozen'. It would therefore seem that at least one British glass manufacturer was issuing these scenic paperweights in the 1860s. Messrs George Davidson of Gateshead probably made other examples late in the 19th-century.

Rarely will a paperweight be found with its original price label or with the name of the retailer. Of extreme rarity are examples bearing the name of the designer or manufacturer. I have a fine early cushion-shaped weight (see Plate 47) three and a half inches long; the back is painted over and on this is

AA

stencilled the title 'Lion de Lucerne' and INVENTEUR within

R & C

crossed laurel branches (the 'R & C' could be 'R & G'). There lies a clue to the 'Inventeur'; who will follow it up? An early oblong scenic weight in the Royal Childrens' Museum at Osborne House, Isle of Wight is marked 'Dopter imp A Paris' and was acquired before 1862 (A. J. V. Dopter patented a method of ornamenting glass in June 1857). I have seen an English view weight of oblong shape and of 20th-century date;

its interest lies in the original paste-on label which reads – 'Reliable series Photographs. Trade Mark W. R. & S. Ltd. E'. Who were W. R. & S. Ltd ?

Today these often charming paperweights can be found in most small antique or second-hand shops. A most interesting collection can be formed at little cost, and will illustrate scenes and times long since past. What a fascinating pictorial picture can be re-created of Victorian times.

A different, but also decorative, type of Victorian glass paperweight are the ball-shaped examples which contain a view and are filled with a liquid in which is suspended snow-like flakes. When the ornament is turned upside down the 'snow' goes to the top; when the weight is returned to the upright position, the 'snow' slowly drifts down with a realistic effect.

Even with inexpensive collectable wares, condition is very important if a worth-while collection is to be formed. Scenic paperweights which have had the prints torn should not be purchased, nor should examples that have been affected by damp. Buy only bright clean specimens and your discrimination will be well rewarded.

47. Typical Victorian scenic paperweights—Lowestoft Pier; Royal Mile, Edinburgh; Bramber, Sussex; 'Lion de Lucerne'. ($3\frac{1}{2}'' \times 2\frac{1}{2}''$)

CHAPTER ELEVEN

GENERAL ADVICE

THE BEST GENERAL advice to collectors is the same whether the purchase price is one or one thousand pounds – buy the best of its type; inferior, damaged examples are dear at any price.

While the collector is endeavouring to master his subject he should at all times be prepared to add to the general fund of knowledge. One of the best ways to do this is to write an article but when doing so it is essential that all hitherto published information should be checked before it is repeated, as it is surprising how many blatant errors are copied by one writer after another.

It does not matter greatly if the article is published or not, as the research that went into its writing will amply repay the collector if the task was undertaken in a conscientious and thorough manner. It is of course advantageous if the article is published in one of the several collector's magazines, for then one's interests are widely publicized and interesting correspondence may result from fellow collectors. New information is often forthcoming from unlikely sources as a result of a published article on a collecting subject.

It is helpful for the new collector to know of his fellow collectors as those already established will naturally be able to give valuable advice both on published information on his chosen subject or on possible sources of supply. The chance of an exchange to mutual advantage is also possible to the collector who prefers to share his interests and information.

The collector should thoroughly concentrate on the period of his subject by reading books, magazines, etc., of the period. Interesting contemporary references can be found to several collecting subjects in such Victorian magazines as the *Art Magazine*. Copies of this are available in several public libraries or may often be purchased reasonably at country house sales. Correspondence with a fellow collector can often obviate fruitless research and duplication of effort.

The question of damage concerns many new and established collectors. Harry Buten of the Buten Museum of Wedgwood at Merion, Pennsylvania, USA, has a neat reply to those who ask if all Wedgwood exhibited is perfect:

If I selected as my friends only those people who are perfect, then I wouldn't have any friends.

When one is collecting purely for financial gain then the answer is reject all damaged articles but if one is collecting for pleasure and to increase one's knowledge then by all means include damaged items (at an appropriate price). Some of my most interesting finds have been damaged and they are none the less interesting for being imperfect.

Chips, small cracks, etc., are normal signs of day to day use and are excusable on rare or documentary pieces. It is quite a different matter to buy ordinary items that have been damaged for one can, with a little patience, find perfect specimens. In recent years the art of china repair has grown to such an extent that resprayed articles can deceive even the expert. It would appear from the way resprayed damaged articles are placed in sale rooms that much of this is done to deceive the purchaser into believing that he is buying a perfect article – this is fraud. Whenever an article is sold as perfect and it proves to have been damaged, it should be returned without delay. It is a wise precaution to insist on a detailed receipt with all purchases; the receipt should state if the piece is sold as perfect, or if not the extent of damage should be stated. With repaired items it should be borne in mind that one is paying for new paint and the repairer's time as well as for the article.

Most experienced collectors will admit that their purchasing mistakes were made when they failed to purchase, rather than when they did. The new collector often misses a never-to-be-repeated opportunity because the price is a little higher than his limit; it is far better to exceed any self-imposed limit when a rare documentary example is found than it is to buy three ordinary specimens at a lower figure. The ordinary pieces can always be purchased but the rarity is perhaps a chance in a lifetime to increase the interest and value of the whole collection.

If the pocket will permit, problem pieces should be purchased; if you are not sure of an object, its maker, period or rarity, it should be purchased and investigated. This is the only way to learn and the investment will seldom be a complete loss.

I have already explained the importance of seeking the help and knowledge of a fellow collector. It is of equal importance to engage the help and advice of a reputable dealer, preferably a specialist in your field. This dealer can, once mutual trust and goodwill are established, be of the greatest help, not only in tracing specimens, but in passing on the benefit of a lifetime's experience. It is in the dealer's interest to steer the new collector clear of pit-falls and to foster his interest and custom. On the collector's part, he must remember that the dealer is a business man. He can only be expected to help the collector who makes an occasional purchase and as the collector proceeds he will find that the dealer becomes more and more essential. Choice specimens from all over the country tend to find their way to specialized dealers and it is their business to try to sell rare objects to the appropriate customer. The better the relationship between a collector and his dealer friend, the more likely the dealer is to notify him of suitable pieces as they arrive. The fact that a prompt payer often has an advantage is a point overlooked by many collectors!

In recent years many antique Fairs have been arranged and have become firmly established – the obvious advantage of these Fairs is that the collector can see, under one roof in one day, the stocks of twenty or more dealers. The dates of these and other Fairs are advertised in collectors magazines and in the National Press. I have purchased several very interesting specimens of Victorian pottery and porcelain at these Fairs.

The touring collector should, apart from seeking the local antiques shops, also visit the local museum. Surprisingly good collections are often to be found in little publicized museums. Naturally, country museums often have key collections of local wares and the Curator is in all probability a mine of information, not only on the objects under his charge, but on other local experts and collectors.

The many 'Stately Homes' that are open to the public during the summer months should not be passed; here again, the collector can often be pleasantly surprised to find pieces illustrative of his interest displayed in their natural contemporary setting. Queen Victoria's residence, Osborne House in the Isle of Wight, should be visited by all collectors of Victoriana and they should not miss the Royal Childrens' Swiss Cottage and Museum situated in the grounds. Lady Bagot's collection at Blithfield Hall, near Rugeley, Staffs includes children's toy tea and dinner services, as well as an interesting collection of children's toys. At least two houses have modern Potteries attached and the visitor can see the basic methods of manufacture. These are at Holkham Hall, Norfolk and at Glynde Place, near Lewes, Sussex. Details of Stately Homes, their location, opening times etc. are contained in an annual inexpensive booklet, 'Historic Houses, Castles and Gardens in Great Britain and Ireland', which is available from most bookshops.

The collector, touring in a district with which he is unfamiliar, may wonder how he is to find the local antique shops with a minimum of trouble. The annual 'International Antiques Yearbook' is of the greatest help in this respect. All classes of dealer are listed, from the leading London Art Dealers, to general antique shops situated in out-of-the-way places. It is the latter class that will especially interest the reader of this book. The 'Antiques Yearbook' should be studied before any collecting tour is contemplated. A series of regional guides has recently been published by A.G.A. Guides under the general title 'Antiques in Britain'. A list of the members of the British Antique Dealers' Association Ltd is also available, price 10/– post free from the Secretary of the Association at 20, Rutland Gate, London, S.W.7.

The modern collector has available to him several magazines which contain interesting, authoritative articles on most branches of collecting – these include 'Antiques Collector'; 'Apollo'; 'Collectors Guide'; 'Connoisseur'; 'Country Life' (weekly). These magazines may be found in many public libraries. For the collector who cannot afford to purchase all these publications, I would suggest that a group of three or four local collectors could each agree to purchase one of the above magazines. These could then be circulated within the 'club'.

The collector should not be afraid to follow his own intuition; it is decidedly to his advantage to collect objects that are out of fashion and therefore available at a low price. In collecting to be out of the fashion is often to be ahead of fashion. This is true of all classes of collecting; a well-known Victorian art collector wrote in his diary for 28th April 1895: 'We went together to the Salon de Champ de Mars, where the Impressionists have their exhibition – some thousand canvases – not one of which one would care to possess.' Those who did care to possess were out of fashion but, as I have said, they were also ahead of fashion. Good hunting.

BIBLIOGRAPHY

This short Bibliography contains only general reference books that are likely to be of help and interest to the reader of this book. Other specialised books are mentioned under the appropriate subject in the book. Several book dealers publish lists or catalogues of collectors books.

The Ceramic Art of Great Britain, L. Jewitt. (1878 and revised edition 1883).

The A.B.C. of Nineteenth Century Pottery and Porcelain, J. F. Blacker. c. 1911.

The A.B.C. of English Saltglaze Stoneware, J. F. Blacker. 1922.

English Country Pottery, R. G. Hagger. 1950.

Handbook of Pottery and Porcelain Marks, J. Cushion and W. B. Honey. 1956.

Victorian Pottery and Porcelain, G. B. Hughes. 1959.

Victoriana, a collector's guide, Violet Wood. 1960.

English and Scottish Earthenware, G. B. Hughes. 1961.

Victorian Porcelain. G. A. Godden, 1961.

19th Century British Glass, H. Wakefield. 1961.

Victorian Pottery, H. Wakefield. 1962.

More Small Decorative Antiques, Therle Hughes. 1962.

British Pottery and Porcelain, 1780–1850, G. A. Godden. 1963.

Encyclopaedia of British Pottery and Porcelain Marks, G. A. Godden. 1964.

Marks and Monograms on European and Oriental Pottery and Porcelain, W. Chaffers. New revised 15th edition. 1965.

INDEX